THE DEMOCRATIC PARTY'S WAR ON MEN:

GYNOCENTRISM

By

Michael Stone

The Democratic Party's War On Men

Copyright © 2014 by Michael Stone

All rights reserved.

Contents

Foreword

Many authors feel that a longer book equals a better book. They fill pages with "fluff" and endless details and descriptions, along with too many statistics and studies just to increase the page count. I disagree. In today's hectic and clustered world of quick text messages, people want the facts in a concise and timely fashion. This book accomplishes just that, giving you everything you need to know with brevity. No useless clutter, no "fluff." This short book will change your view of American politics forever.

Introduction

I'm not going to paint with a broad brush and lump all women together. If I did, it would be complete hypocrisy, because this is exactly what the feminists and gynocentrists do—lump all men together.

This book is an attempt at the exact opposite; true understanding of equality and fairness for *everyone*. If you're a woman, please let your guard down and read this book objectively. Women are not all the same. Their political views are as diverse as men's political views. This book does not apply to all women. Actually, it is about the *manipulation* of women by the Democratic Party.

The Democratic Party has become the party of hate, pitting whites against blacks, women against men, rich against poor, and believers against atheists. Wherever a wedge can be inserted between the American people, the Democratic Party is driving it in, carefully polarizing the people. If the people are busy fighting amongst themselves, they're not paying attention to the ultimate goal of Washington politicians—getting rich off of the American people's tax money.

This book is not about anyone's agenda, nor an endorsement of any person or party. It is a call for justice. If you want to dismiss me as a woman hater, there isn't much I can do about that. But you would have to completely ignore the facts to reach that conclusion.

I only ask one thing as you read this book: Remember the Golden Rule. If it was done to you, would you like it?

The Equal Protection Clause of the Constitution is routinely violated by the Democratic Party for a very deliberate cause—keep the people fighting amongst themselves, confused, chasing red herrings, angry, polarized, and filled with an artificially inspired hate. As we hate each other, they quietly rob the bank and leave the country a little worse every day.

Gynocentrism

Gyno-centrism: The pursuit of *selective* equal rights. When the right is of advantage to women, it must be enforced to the maximum extent of the law. If the right is undesirable to women, it is considered an undue burden and cannot be enforced. The Equal Protection Clause of the Constitution only applies as women *feel* it should.

* * *

Women can never be held accountable for any action or crime when committed against a male. The root cause of all evil is men, and women are merely responding to this universal truth. When a woman commits a crime against another female, she was likely abused by a man at some point and therefore isn't really responsible.

* * *

A woman's refusal to accept fairness or equality in matters of law or gender relations.

Gynocentric Keywords

Man: Two testicles and a Y chromosome.

Sexual Harassment: When a man tells a dirty joke or flirts. If a woman tells the same joke or flirts, it *does not* fall into the sexual harassment category. Women can never be found guilty of this, even if they display extreme sexual behavior towards men. A tool for removing men from positions of power and replacing them with liberal women.

Equal Pay Doctrine: The law that states companies must pay women the same as men as long as they hold the same title as a male counterpart. They do not have to work as many hours as he does or perform as well. Used during every election by the Democrats to rally women, but never actually fixed, even when the Democrats have controlled the Presidency, the Congress, and Senate for years. The imaginary pay gap must always be asserted in order to get votes. In cases where women earn more than men, this data must be ignored.

Discrimination: Something that occurs when a liberal woman doesn't get what she wants. A woman can never be found guilty of discriminating against a man.

Equality: Women must have every right and advantage as men do. This does not apply the other way around; men do not get every right and advantage of women.

The Constitution: A vague reference point. If liberal women agree with a particular section, it is a concrete right. If liberal women disagree with a part of it, the document was written hundreds of years ago by oppressive men and is out of touch with modern times.

Abortion: Women, and only women, will decide who lives and who dies. Men can have no control in the decision. If the woman decides the child will be born, the man must pay her a significant part of his pay for eighteen years.

Hate: Any opinion different than yours.

Chapter 1: The Birth of Feminism

It would be intellectually dishonest to pretend women didn't have legitimate grievances. Throughout most of history, women were almost second-class citizens. Women were allowed the role of housewife and little more, with the exception of those born into royalty, wealth, or influential families. They were expected to make clothes, sew, store and preserve food, cook, clean the home, raise the children, and perhaps even care for all the livestock on a farm. Women were typically subservient to their husband.

On July 19 and 20, 1848, some women decided they had had enough and held a convention in Seneca Falls, New York. Hundreds of women showed up. Some signed a "Declaration of Sentiments and Resolutions." The demands were reasonable: The right to own property, wages, money, access to education, access to professional careers, and the right to vote—essentially the same rights afforded to men. Who could argue against this? Everyone should have equal opportunities in this world. This is why feminism eventually succeeded in these demands. There was no rational or moral basis to deny people these things.

But there is one phrase in the "Declaration of Sentiments and Resolutions" that gives us a preview of the ugly direction feminism was destined for. It reads, "The history of mankind is a history of repeated injuries and usurpations on the part of man against woman."

Talk about lumping all men together. In their words, all men were guilty of injuring all women. No man ever treated his wife well. No man ever treated any woman well. There is only one common history between all men and women—all men injuring women in some way. If this was true, when a man asked to marry a woman, wouldn't the answer always be "No?"

After succeeding in getting the rights of property ownership, keeping their wages, the right to vote, and all the rights afforded to men, feminism quieted down but never went away. They won! What could they fight for now?

Feminism actually shifted away from women with legitimate grievances, who lived under harsh conditions, to college campuses. Now, the average "oppressed woman" grew up in an upper- or middle-class family. Tuition was paid for them. They sat comfortably on grass lawns sharing their stories of "hardship" and "terrible lives." Certainly, men were to blame for all their dissatisfaction. The original feminists won their battle, and therefore, they could win theirs.

But what would they fight for? They had equal rights in every way. This is when the pursuit of *extra* or *special* rights began. The only way to true happiness was to have special protections, in order to "level the playing field" with all the oppressive men. But it was a slow battle. Most women just weren't interested. The majority of women wanted to go about their work and business, find the right man, and have a happy family. This frustrated the feminists into a raging anger. They were unhappy, which meant every woman was supposed to be unhappy! So, they started the gender war to suck in many levelheaded women.

They would take legitimate issues and turn them into "female-only" problems. And all issues became a crisis at their particular time in the spotlight: Abortion, college admissions, discrimination, sexual harassment, date-rape, and equal pay. All of these issues have one important thing in common—when the discussions and court cases were over, women emerged with extra rights that men don't have. *I will document these special rights extensively throughout this book, and show how the Democratic Party is the major force behind this.*

Yes, feminism started with legitimate grievances and abuses. But pushing the pendulum too far the other way is not a cure or a remedy. It just creates the same problems for other people. If you are a man hater, then you probably enjoy seeing men denied rights that women have and receiving unequal treatment by the United States government. But reflect on this for a moment: We have all told someone at some time or another, "Two wrongs don't make a right." How about following your own advice?

Chapter 2: The Birth of Gynocentrism

There is an important distinction between gynocentrism and feminism; where feminists originally fought for equal rights in all areas of life, the gynocentric movement fights for rights that are exclusive to women. Gynocentrism is actually a female-worshiping religion. There are many groups that help women connect with "Their inner goddess." (I will talk more about that in a later case study.) Essentially, the world rotates around women.

Nothing is a problem until it affects women. For example, there are constant fundraisers and government efforts to stop violence against women. But there has never been one fundraiser or government effort to stop violence against men.

Even though men are far more likely to die from violence, and are the victims of domestic violence almost 40 percent of the time, the U.S. government and gynocentrists refuse to even acknowledge that women are very capable of violence. Did you know that in two-thirds of child abuse cases, the abuser was female?

The government passed the **Violence Against Women Act** in 1994. Even though men are far more likely to be the victim of some form of violence, there is no Violence Against Men Act. The Democratic Party will block it the minute someone tries to pass it. Remember, with gynocentrism, only the woman can be the victim.

14

Have you ever seen feminists marching to stop the killing of young men in Chicago? Have you seen them marching to stop the killing of young men in Detroit, Los Angeles, New York, or Atlanta? No, you haven't seen them march anywhere for any man. It's only a problem when a woman is affected. The Democrats constantly talk about domestic violence against women. Have you ever heard even one Democrat speak about violence against men? No, you haven't, have you?

You may be asking some obvious questions right about now. Questions like, "If there are men in the Democratic Party, why would they go along with this?" The answer is simple. Women make up the majority of the population in the United States. For those of you who are terrible in math, it simply means there are a lot more women in America than men.

These men in the Democratic Party know a simple fact: They have to take rights away from men and give extra rights to women in order to get elected. Feminists exclusively vote Democrat. The deal was signed in blood years ago between the feminists and Democratic politicians—give us everything we want, and we will deliver millions upon millions of votes.

Women are the largest demographic in the Democratic Party. Without the female vote, Democrats can't win an election. This is how the Gynocentric Movement was born. It was a marriage of sociopaths.

I will discuss the many extra rights women have throughout this book. But for now, let's look at the most glaring example first—abortion.

The decision of whether a human being will live or die rests exclusively with the female. The father of the child has no say either way. If the mother wants the child, and he wishes to abort, only her decision is respected by the courts.

If the mother wants to abort and the father wants to raise the child, he has no legal rights and can only watch as his son or daughter is killed. However, if the mother decides the child will be born, even against the father's wishes, the courts will order him to give the mother a substantial part of his pay for at least eighteen years. The same court that blocks him from having any say in the child's existence, will now order him to pay child support. If he doesn't, the government will come to his home with guns and drag him off to jail.

In Florida, a young man decided to exercise *his right to choose*. He tricked his girlfriend into taking an abortion pill. She believed it was an antibiotic. As expected, she miscarried.

Here are the particulars: "ORLANDO, Florida (Reuters) - A Florida man who admitted to tricking his pregnant girlfriend into taking pills known to cause abortion has been ordered to serve more than 13 years in federal prison and to pay her about $28,500 in restitution, U.S. prosecutors said. John Andrew Welden, 29, was sentenced on Monday…"

If his girlfriend didn't want the child, she could walk into an abortion clinic and end the pregnancy. There would be no consequences for her. The staff would comfort her and tell her everything would be okay. She made the right choice. But

Mr. Welden exercised the exact same "choice" and was sentenced to thirteen years in federal prison.

Is that Equal Protection of the Law as ordered by the U.S. Constitution? Of course not! And the government knows it's not. But if anyone tries to change the laws, to make them more equal, prominent Democrats across the country accuse them of "hating women."

If you try to take away extra rights from women, that equals hate with the Democrats. But it gets even better. If the mother marries a millionaire, and the father is living in poverty, he still has to pay her a substantial part of his paycheck. You will never see this situation in reverse; the father with custody of the child, married to a millionaire, and the mother who didn't want the baby living in poverty, paying the father a large chunk of her pay.

Can you imagine if the situation were reversed? The man decided if the child would be born, it was, he took custody of the baby, and the mother had to pay him substantial support for eighteen years. Women would be setting themselves on fire and jumping off of bridges to protest this "oppression." But the Democratic Party fights relentlessly to keep things this way, because it guarantees them millions of female votes.

There are thousands of men paying child support and being denied visitation by the mother. The courts rarely take serious action in these cases. But if the father stops paying her, off to jail he goes. You would be hard pressed to find even one woman who is paying a man child support, and he is denying her visitation. Women can easily get a restraining order on the child's father, with a mere allegation and no proof. A man can never get a restraining order against a woman with just an allegation. This is the core of gynocentrism; the woman must have protections the man doesn't get.

With no proof of threat, just her word, the father can't see his children, maybe even for years. Never is a mother denied visitation simply because the father made an allegation against her. Often, fathers become frustrated and just give up.

The mother has more children with someone else and still collects the first father's money. In the end, the children suffer the most. All children deserve to be raised by *both* of their parents, but the Democratic Party needs votes, so to hell with the children and to hell with the Equal Protection guaranteed by the Constitution. The Democratic Party has declared war on men.

Case Study: Inequality in Clubs and Institutions

One of the main goals of gynocentrism is to destroy all male institutions and replace them with female institutions. They are succeeding. But why would they even bother with this? Why would they care if a bunch of men have a political group, a men's golf course, a men's-only health club, or any group that is exclusive to men? The answer is simple. There is strength in numbers. You can't allow men to be united in anything. That is a threat to gynocentrism. Only women can have groups that are exclusive to them (to level the playing field, of course).

Over the years, through lawsuits and Democratic Party intervention, all male clubs or institutions are being brought down. Ironically, as the male institutions are being taken down, the female-only institutions are bursting into mainstream America.

The message is clear: Women can have clubs and institutions that exclusively serve them, but if men attempt to have anything without female involvement, it is discrimination. This is the heart and soul of gynocentrism.

Women need to have extra rights to keep the world in order. If women don't want men in an institution, it's because they are all evil and a distraction for the women's mission. Are you having trouble believing that the situation could be this insane?

Here are just a few examples of institutions that allow only women:

Curves: The nationwide fitness network will only allow women in their facilities. No men are allowed, period. There are no fitness corporations that only allow men. There may be some random gym tailored to men, but as soon as a woman files a complaint, they will be forced to admit her. A man has started a fitness network modeled after Curves, but for men. It is almost certain he will be sued and forced to admit women at some point. Curves will not have this problem.

National Women's Political Caucus: A group whose sole mission is to get female candidates elected. They will likely let a man donate money or spend his time helping them, but will not endorse any male candidate unless there are no female candidates. Then, they will only back a man if he has sworn allegiance to gynocentrism and will take rights from men. There are no political organizations that focus on helping men get elected. They would be sued immediately for discrimination. No male-centered groups are allowed by the Democratic Party and their legion of lawyers and legal activists.

Women-Only Health Centers: A local paper in the New England area displayed a large ad for a new health center called, "All Women Health Care." The ad actually boasted they only hire female doctors. There are many health centers like this around the country, ones that exclude male doctors and boast about it. They merely have to claim that women are "more comfortable" with a female, and they get a free pass to discriminate. Male doctors could never get away with conduct like this.

Professional Sports: Anyone who watches professional sports will routinely see female reporters broadcasting to the media in men's locker rooms after games. They were *forced* to allow women into men's locker rooms. Some female reporters have claimed "harassment" while in the locker room, because someone made them uncomfortable. Can you believe the absurdity of this? Demanding to go into a male locker room, and then claiming outrage because you didn't like what you saw. You will never see a male reporter in a female athlete's locker room. All men are predators. Do you see the pattern over and over? What is unacceptable from men is completely acceptable for women. This is gynocentrism in action.

Emily's List: This is one of the largest Political Action Committees in the United States, with over two million members. Emily's list only supports pro-choice women. Men need not apply. Can you imagine if a Political Action Committee was formed to only support Catholic men? Women couldn't apply for any funds. The group would be sued instantly, and the courts would issue injunctions to cease and desist. There would be scathing headlines in all the mainstream media that "sexism" was alive and well. But female politicians can openly discriminate against men with no consequences. This is the left's version of "equality." There are many female-only organizations across America.

Here is a critical point to remember: There are still some men-only golf courses, or social clubs, but they are few in number. One by one, a woman sues, and the club is forced to admit women. Even when it is a private club, the government always finds some kind of "public usage" loophole, such as "You once held a public tournament; therefore, you are a public entity." Pure nonsense, but it often forces the club to admit women. Men sometimes sue female clubs like Curves, but they always lose. One man actually sued Hooter's, claiming he could be a server there. It's absurd, and he should have lost. But, you can be certain if a restaurant or chain had high paying server jobs for only male models, and a woman claimed discrimination, she would win, and either receive a job or a cash settlement.

Still skeptical? Consider this: A golf club in Haverhill, Massachusetts was sued by the female members. They claimed the men got better "tee times" and easier memberships (Oh, the oppression. How did they make it through that nightmare?) Well, the poor downtrodden women got millions! Millions, because they didn't like their "tee time." With the real suffering out there, and real legal cases where people lose everything and get stiffed, this is what the courts find important.

Can you name one case where men felt they were being treated unfairly and got millions? No, you can't, because it has never happened. If the courts are unbiased, how is it that women constantly win discrimination cases and men virtually never do? The answer is simple; only women can be the victims. Male institutions are severely punished for excluding women, but female institutions continue on, unscathed.

Chapter 3: Sexual Harassment: Power through Victimization

No tool has been as effective as sexual harassment in changing the political landscape. It is a weapon exclusively for women. It has ended the careers of many, many men. It has never ended the career of a woman. It is the ultimate trump card in the Democratic Party's play book. However, men in the Democratic Party are granted immunity by the feminists and gynocentrists. The Democratic Party is their sugar-daddy, and they can't bite the hand that feeds them. Ironically, it is usually the Democrat men who walk all over women.

Bill Clinton behaved like a sexual predator, with a twenty-year history of misogyny and using his position of power to get sex, even with interns young enough to be his daughter. The feminists never uttered a word about good old Billy boy. He gave them extra rights and that is all that mattered.

Anthony Weiner exposed himself over and over. Still, the feminists had nothing to say. Only when the pictures and story went nationwide did they jump on the bandwagon.

The mayor of San Diego, Bob Filner, was so comfortable as a Democrat that he would physically grab women and touch or kiss them. It wasn't until woman after woman came forward with allegations that he was finally pressured to step down. If he hadn't been a Democrat, he would have been gone long before that.

The Kennedy's had a long and sordid history with women, but the mainstream, Democrat-controlled media still refers to them as American royalty. Even when a compelling rape case was brought against William Kennedy Smith, the feminists were completely silent.

In the American legal system, women are virtually never found guilty of sexual harassment. There are well-documented cases where female bosses repeatedly make unwanted sexual advances, men file charges, and then they lose the case every time. One of the major networks did an investigative report on this legal bias. They showed a case where the female boss wore earrings shaped like a penis, made graphic sexual comments to her male subordinate, and propositioned him. Of course, authorities refused to take any action. Can you imagine if a male boss had a tie with a naked woman on it and propositioned his secretary? She wouldn't even have to file anything, because he would be fired immediately.

A female acquaintance once complained of the following: A female manager at a large company would often sit on the desk of a shy young man. She would take out a lollipop and lick it suggestively, while staring into his face and making suggestive comments. There was usually a crowd of women around. The young man's face would turn beet red. One of the women approached him privately, telling him he should file a complaint. He told her he would never win. He was right, and the offending manager knew he would never win. That is why she was so comfortable humiliating him in public. She knew women aren't held to the same standard as men. The young man soon quit his job. If a male manager sat on a woman's desk licking a lollipop suggestively, he would be fired that day.

Here is a case that happened in a Massachusetts hospital. A male registered nurse was hired and placed on a floor with only one other male registered nurse. As the new nurse reported in the morning, the nurses would slander the other male nurse relentlessly. The manager even took part in it. Each day, they looked for things to get the senior male nurse in trouble. One of the nurses even said, "Oh, they're out to get Joe" right in public. There was no fear. After several months of attacking him, they succeeded in getting him fired.

As soon as the first male nurse was gone, they immediately began harassing the newly hired male nurse. One afternoon, he was bending over to get supplies out of a closet, and a nurse's aide walked up, stood with her crotch in his face, and said, "Hey, while you're down there, ha ha." Then they would trace his every move, looking for anything to write him up for. One of the *female* nurses made a potentially life-threatening mistake, failing to discontinue a blood thinner, and the nurse manager quickly told the male nurse not to report it. Shortly after, the male nurse was reported and written up for not triple documenting that he had given a Fleets enema. A female nurse makes a life-threatening mistake, and it is quickly covered up. Compare that to the male nurse who gave a routine, over-the-counter treatment to a patient, documented it twice, yet it was written up for a "medication error."

The group of women continued to make his life miserable. He called the Director of Nurses and told the secretary he was in a harassment situation and he was desperate. She did not reply. He called over and over for weeks, as his very ability to take care of his family was being threatened. The Director of Nurses never took any action. She never even replied. It was just a male nurse; they had no protection in her eyes. The ladies were having fun ruining another man's life. Why should she interfere with that?

The harassment continued. There was a culture of "This is a women's world. We will do what we want to men, and no one will do anything." If he even failed to initial one box, he was reported for a medication error. Female nurses could miss initialing twenty boxes and were only asked to sign them later.

With nowhere else to turn, he filed a complaint with the Massachusetts Commission Against Discrimination. The "Commission" never investigated. Instead, they just asked the nurse manager and Director of Nurses, "Oh, are you harassing the only male registered nurse on this floor?" They simply had to deny it, and the case went away.

Ironically, around the same time, a female nurse's aide complained when a male nurse's aide made a dirty joke. The State of Massachusetts had investigators in the building at eleven o'clock at night interrogating him and others. Two male nurses are degraded and harassed out of their jobs, file a complaint, and no one ever looks into it. But a male makes a dirty joke and investigators are in the building late at night leaving no stone unturned.

Can you imagine if the women who were hired in an engineering firm with all men, were degraded, and a man put his crotch in one of their faces and said, "Hey, while you're down there." Then the men target their performance and make their job nearly impossible. They desperately call the CEO and file a complaint. They even have to leave their jobs to escape the harassment. It would be on the national news, feminists would be marching, and the men would be fired for this outrageous, criminal conduct. The women would receive multi-million dollar settlements. But, when the same thing happens to a man, there is no penalty. In all situations, the first law of gynocentrism applies: Only women can be the victims!

Let's take a look at how sexual harassment has been used effectively against men. The first high profile case that comes to mind is Clarence Thomas. The Democratic Party didn't want him on the Supreme Court. So, like the Democrats so often do, they set out to destroy his name. They decided on playing the sexual harassment card. A woman named Anita Hill suddenly "comes forward" accusing him of sexual misconduct towards her. It supposedly happened about ten years earlier. Why didn't she say anything before he was nominated to the nation's highest court? Why was it suddenly an issue then?

Throughout the proceedings, lawyers sat beside Anita Hill and coached her on what to say. If she was simply telling the truth, she wouldn't need feminist lawyers coaching her. Her testimony was so inconsistent that Senator Arlen Spector accused her of flat out perjury. People saw through the hoax, and Clarence Thomas was confirmed. But his name was forever smeared, and the feminists never apologized for putting him through months of public humiliation.

If a man accused Ruth Bader Ginsburg of sexually harassing him, do you think there would be hearings like that? Of course not. It would be laughed away. If that isn't a double-standard, what is?

More recently, it was used again against a conservative black man who ran for president of the United States, Herman Cain. The Democrats have a history of this, and all logic points to them as the ones behind the charges. One of the women even has feminist activist, Gloria Allred, representing her (a little suspicious, by anyone's standards). Unfortunately, this time, they succeeded.

Women continued to accuse him of sexual harassment until he finally dropped out of the race. He said his family couldn't take anymore. Of course, as soon as he dropped out of the race, all the allegations suddenly stopped. While he was running, women kept coming forward. When he quit the race, no more women came forward. This is so transparent and hurts women who really do get sexually harassed. But, who cares about justice and decency? Do what you have to do to get what you want.

Apparently, there is no age requirement with gynocentrists. They even hate little boys. In Denver, a six-year-old boy kissed a little girl's hand. He was suspended for sexual harassment. You're reading this correctly; he was suspended for sexual harassment for kissing a little girl's hand. First grader, Hunter Yelton, was branded a sexual harasser and suspended from school by the female principal. This principal was likely indoctrinated with hate on her college campus. If a six-year-old girl kissed a little boy's hand, do you think that female principal would have suspended her for sexual harassment? Of course not. She would smile and say, "Isn't she sweet."

That woman must be seething with hate to do that to a six-year-old boy who has no concept of what sex is. If a sixteen-year-old girl grabbed a boy's crotch in front of that same principal, nothing would be done about it. Fortunately, the case got national media attention on Fox News, and the backlash was so intense that they changed the "charge" to inappropriate conduct. It's still ridiculous, but better than being branded a sex offender at age six.

Clearly, there is an agenda behind this insanity. They want every male tattooed as a sex offender from birth. It gives them more power. They want all males cowering in fear of women, terrified of that all-powerful trump card that women can play to destroy them at any time. It doesn't matter if the man actually did it. The woman *only has to say he did it.* There doesn't even have to be a clear definition of what constitutes "harassment;" the woman merely has to feel "uncomfortable" and the man (or little boy) is found guilty.

Think about the incredible double-standard that is now the legal standard in America—women can be as sexually explicit as they want, can touch or humiliate a man in public, and there are no legal consequences. But when a six-year-old boy kisses a girl's hand, it is a sex crime. The Democrats, feminists, and gynocentrists worked for decades to completely hijack the legal system.

Here is yet another case that boggles the mind and proves that gynocentrism is running rampant. In 2002, high school football star, Brian Banks, had a promising future. He had agreed to play football for the University of Southern California and was considered a potential professional football player. Then, classmate, Wanetta Gibson, claimed he dragged her into a stairwell and raped her.

Based on her testimony, he was sent to prison for five years. Gibson received over one million dollars in a settlement from the school district, claiming it was "unsafe." After Banks was released from prison, Gibson contacted him on Facebook, met with him, and apologized for fabricating the story that ruined his life. Banks secretly recorded Gibson's confession. His conviction was overturned, but no charges were ever filed against Wanetta Gibson.

She spent over a million dollars from the legal settlement, living in luxury, while Banks sat in a prison for something he didn't do. Even with a taped confession from Gibson, she was never charged with anything.

It gets even better. Gibson blew through the money and ended up on welfare, with two kids from different fathers. She was actually ordered to pay child support but then got out of that, because she didn't have a job. Men go to prison for failure to pay child support, whether they have a job or not. However, the state has decided not to prosecute her for either lying about rape or failure to pay child support. No double-standard there?

If a man sent a woman to prison, was later caught on tape admitting he committed perjury to send her there, and had filed false reports to do it, that man would be arrested immediately. But Gibson is still walking free. How did the system get this perverted? Is it just legal chaos and incompetence causing these kinds of discrepancies in the way justice is administered? No, it isn't chaos or incompetence. As I have proved, and will continue to prove, the Democratic Party has fought for years to create a special class of "rights" and even "immunity" for women. Even when women file false charges against men, they are immune from prosecution.

They want women to know it is okay to falsely accuse men of sexual harassment or rape.

If you feel this is far-fetched, consider these words, "Men who are unjustly accused of rape can sometimes gain from the experience." Catherine Comins, Vassar College Assistant Dean of Student Life, as quoted in *Time Magazine*, June 3, 1991. Really? A man goes to prison for something he doesn't do, and he can *gain* from the experience. This is pure hatred.

Ms. Comins influenced thousands of female students at her college, almost encouraging man haters to file a rape charge. It's inconceivable to imagine an assistant dean warping the minds of young, impressionable college students. But, this kind of gynocentric/feminist hatred is rampant on college campuses across America.

As I stated earlier, college campuses are one of the main recruiting grounds of the Democratic Party. They need to fill our next generation with the same hate they feel, because it helps win elections. The more allegations of sexual harassment and rape, the better, because the Democratic Party gets to rush in as the "savior" and grant more special rights and immunities. The party of hate will do anything to win an election.

Case Study: Finding Your Inner Goddess

If you're still skeptical about gynocentrism, still doubting that people could be that self-centered and bigoted, then look no further than the movement to "find your inner goddess." This sounds silly and harmless, but is actually another way of cultivating women and indoctrinating them into gynocentrism and complete self-absorption.

"It's all about *you,* because *you* are a goddess, and *you* deserve the best of everything. And if *you* aren't getting everything *you* ever wanted, then someone is holding *you* down. *You* need to get in touch with *your* inner goddess."

Many of these groups also encourage women to get in touch with their "inner-bitch," because *you* get more of what *you* want by being "a bitch." You'll notice there is never any reference to the greater community-at-large, what's good for "us."

A quick search on the internet will bring up dozens upon dozens of sites that help women "find their inner goddess." There are countless gurus who can show you the way to your "divine self." Not to mention all the books on the subject. Many focus on shallow goals, like beauty, and some with a little more substance, like improving your well-being, although the way to improving your well-being is usually some female empowerment-type program. Other sites equate sexual liberation with becoming a goddess. In short, being sexually promiscuous is what women should strive for to achieve true happiness. Whether it's simply beauty, or self-esteem, or flat-out casual sex the sites promote, they all have one common thread—you are a goddess simply because of your gender. Character, morals, or achievements count for little. Just celebrate your "female deity."

Another quick search on the internet, or even a bookstore, will help women "Get in touch with their inner bitch." On one site, a psychologist gives multiple ways that women can achieve this. We all know the world would be a much better place if women would just let that inner bitch out. One author recommends getting rid of "toxic niceness," because "nice is a four-letter word."

Of course, there is the excuse as to why you need to become even more aggressive and self-centered. It's to counter years of repression. Let go of those manners your parents and teachers taught you; that was repression. Find your inner goddess and become a bitch. Then everything will work out perfectly. This goes hand in hand with gynocentrism, the female-worshipping religion; with its very own altar in the Democratic Party.

Chapter 4: The Media and Gynocentrism

You may ask, "What does the media have to do with the Democratic Party's war on men?" Many of you already know the answer to this question. But, for those of you who don't, the answer is, "The media has *everything* to do with the Democratic Party's war on men."

It is common knowledge and well documented that the liberal left controls most of the mainstream media (roughly 85 percent of their staff vote Democrat). Here is just a partial list of media outlets firmly in the hands of the Democrats: PBS (Public Broadcasting System), CNN, MSNBC, ABC, NBC, CBS, Time Magazine, Newsweek, Bravo, Lifetime, The New York Times, and any magazine or television station run by Oprah Winfrey. Again, this is only a partial list. If I mentioned all the major newspapers, it would fill pages.

When Hollywood has a fundraiser, it is always to raise money for the Democrats. Many A-list celebrities campaign for the Democrats each election. George Clooney held a $40,000 per plate fundraiser for the Democrats in the 2012 presidential election. There were scores of high-powered actors and producers, including Leonardo DiCaprio, Cameron Diaz, Jerry Seinfeld, Ben Stiller, Ben Affleck, and many others. High-powered producers like Steven Spielberg and Jeffrey Katzenberg are huge donors, and they are two of the major forces keeping Hollywood as the propaganda arm of the Democrats. Clearly, many actors suck up to the power players in Hollywood to further their careers. Support the party, or pay a price.

Tom Selleck took a conservative stance and was attacked on national television by Rosie O'Donnell. Some conservative actors have complained that they have to hide the fact they aren't Democrats. Patricia Heaton, star of *Everyone Loves Raymond*, came right out and said, "Her conservative views have hurt her career." Sounds like the old Soviet Union, doesn't it? Speak out against the KGB, and you pay a heavy price.

Bill Maher gave one million dollars to a Democratic Party Political Action Committee. Around the same time, Maher called Sarah Palin a " C...t" and a "Twut," because she opposed Democratic Party policies. There was no backlash from the media or Democrats. But isn't there a *"War on Women?"* He called her the most degrading name a woman can be humiliated by, all because he didn't like her political views. He tried to suppress and intimidate her into silence and deprive her of a free opinion.

Where were the feminists? They remained silent, just like they remain silent when Democrats sexually harass women. Give the gynocentrists special rights, and you get the keys to the henhouse. There was never any boycott or action against him. The networks and liberal media gave him a free pass, because he was a Democrat.

Ironically, a woman named Sandra Fluke testified before Congress that other people should pay thousands of dollars for women's birth control (notice no mention of paying for men's birth control, since that would be against gynocentrism). She wanted to be as sexually active as she wanted, at no cost to herself.

But when non-Democrat, Rush Limbaugh, called Sandra Fluke a "slut," there was immediate outrage across the mainstream media. There were boycotts and pressure was put on every station that aired him. His comments were mild compared to Bill Maher. But old Rush wasn't a member of the party.

How about Martin Bashir, the MSNBC host, who said someone should defecate on Sarah Palin (another class act in the Democratic Party's attack dog ranks). Again, the left wing media did not criticize Bashir. No boycotts, no pressure. Bashir eventually resigned when he knew his credibility had been lost. But the president of MSNBC thanked him and called him a "…good man and respected colleague." Do you think he would describe Rush Limbaugh that way? If Bashir said someone should defecate on Hillary Clinton, he would be fired that afternoon!

Here is some more evidence of the marriage between Hollywood and the Democratic Party. At least **sixty-six** Hollywood donors are sending money to Kentucky to try and unseat Senator Mitch McConnell. The list includes producers, agents, lawyers, and celebrities like Danny DeVito, Jack Black, Jon Hamm, Nicolas Cage, and many others. Why would they care about a state that is thousands of miles away from them? What does Kentucky have to do with their jet-set lifestyles? They care, because the Democratic Party and the high-powered movie producers tell them what to think. Likely, most are trying to further their careers. You'll notice most of the A-list actors who are visible supporters of the

Democrats get many high-paying roles. This is American democracy? A small group of millionaires influencing elections all around the country, only to serve their own selfish interests, is considered democracy? No, it's a small group of wealthy people forcing their opinions on millions of Americans.

For you die-hard Democratic Party supporters, here is yet another example of in-your-face bias and outright bigotry. An actress named Stacey Dash posted support for Mitt Romney on her Twitter account. The explosion of outright hate from the liberal-left was astonishing.

She was asked to "…kill herself," called racial slurs (she is part black), told she was "…slutting herself to the white man," called an "indoor slave," and every profanity you can imagine. All those verbal attacks were because she said she was voting against the Democrats. She is a well-known actress, and the left-wing media wanted to shout her down as quick as possible. The "tolerant" Democrats who accuse everyone else of hate, launched the most hate-filled attack on this woman all because she wouldn't march in lock-step with them.

Again, the feminists and gynocentrists were silent. Not one of them stood up for a fellow woman; nor did they stand up for her right to a free opinion, and her right to vote her preference. Shouldn't they be outraged? Bill Maher calls Sarah Palin a "C...t," and Bill Maher calls Sarah Palin a "Twut," simply because she wants to have her own views. Martin Bashir says "…someone should defecate on Sarah Palin." All this hate is directed at women by Democrats. Not a word from anyone in the Democratic Party. Can you see the incredible hypocrisy here? The very people degrading women are accusing others of "A War on Women." No one dared speak up; Hollywood and the Democratic Party would destroy their careers overnight.

Here is another interesting fact: Even though Concerned Women for America is a much bigger organization than the National Organization for Women, the media never goes to them for a quote or opinion on a story. They only ask for NOW's opinion. Why would they ignore the largest women's organization? Because NOW is affiliated with the Democratic Party and liberal feminists, CWFA is not.

There is a method to their madness. They only quote radical feminists for a reason. They are sending a message to women, and it's a message that says, "All women are anti-man and pro-abortion. If you think differently, you're an outcast." Only giving one group airtime clearly meets the threshold of propaganda. The Democratic Party has worked long and hard to control the mainstream media. Don't expect any changes in the near future.

Now, let's get into the gynocentric messages Hollywood pumps into homes and movie theatres across America, and even overseas. Here is one of the cardinal rules of Hollywood's gynocentrism: Violence against men is acceptable, even healthy, when a woman commits it. But violence against women, under any circumstances, is unacceptable, even if a man is defending himself.

Every year, Hollywood pumps out multiple carbon copies of the same plot—husband/boyfriend is abusive, woman tries to get away, finds a new boyfriend while she is on the run, old abusive boyfriend finds her, then she kills him with a gun or whatever she can find. Everyone lives happily ever after. The abusive boyfriend is always killed, and the woman is always justified in doing it. Here is a partial list of the better known ones:

Safe Haven

Enough

Double Jeopardy

Delores Clairborne

Sleeping With The Enemy

The Burning Bed

There have been multitudes of television shows and movies with the same message. Oddly enough, there has never been a movie where the man kills his wife/girlfriend in self-defense and everyone lives happily ever after. Why are there dozens of movies where the woman is justified in killing an abusive man, but no movies where a man is justified in killing an abusive woman?

Forty percent of domestic violence cases are caused by abusive women. That translates into millions of real cases. Not one single movie where the abusive woman gets killed by the man. Hollywood's message is clear. Violence by women against men is acceptable. Violence by men against women, even if she is twice his size and a known psychopath, is never acceptable.

You will also notice women assaulting men on television and in the movies constantly, and the theme is "He deserved it." Even if he says something she doesn't like, she can slap him, punch him in the face, or hit him over the head with something. Again, no matter how evil the woman is, the man is never justified in hitting her...even if she hit him first! This is not coincidental. Hollywood is very conscious of every move they make. For one thing, their largest demographic is women, and they assume all women are man haters who enjoy seeing men being hit. Secondly, they know the rules of the Democratic Party and gynocentrism: **only women can be the victims.**

You may think this is harmless when you hear someone say, "Oh, it's only in the movies." But this propaganda has helped many real women kill their husbands, claim abuse, and walk away free— even after shooting their defenseless husband in the back. No man ever shot his wife in the back, claimed he was abused, and was later found innocent. Gynocentrism is deadly, and absolutely real.

Gynocentrism even has a network of its own. It's called "Lifetime." Anyone who watches this network gets an endless parade of husbands who are abusive, cheaters, and rapists. On one particular Father's Day, Lifetime actually aired a movie about a father who molested his daughter (A Long Way Home). This is the sickness of Hollywood. Their idea of a Father's Day tribute is a man who molests his own daughter? But that is the gynocentric message: all men are rapists and abusers. Of course, on Mother's Day, there were no movies about women mistreating their children, just saintly women who sacrificed all for the kids.

Finally, one last "smoking gun" that even rabid Democrats can't hide from: During the Federal Government shutdown in October 2013, all three major networks, ABC, CBS, and NBC, blamed the Republicans forty-one times for the shutdown. Not once did they say the Democrats were responsible. Not one time! This is unbiased reporting?

How can they blame the Republicans forty-one times and never the Democrats even once? These "reporters" know damn well what the producers want to hear. If they say anything against the Democrats, they are out of a job. It is blatantly obvious to anyone who can think for themselves that the mainstream media is clearly in bed with the Democratic Party. Liberals may not be bothered by this. But this is the first step to a totalitarian dictatorship. Whether it's China or any other totalitarian regime in the world, they have one thing in common: they keep the media firmly in their grip and punish dissidents swiftly. This is where the Democrats are taking America.

Chapter 5: Equal Pay Propaganda

The Equal Pay Act was signed into law on June 10, 1963. For fifty years, it has been illegal to pay someone more simply because of their gender. There isn't a single company anywhere in the United States which has a higher pay scale for men. If any company paid men more than women for no logical reason, hoards of lawyers would be stumbling over each other as they raced to file a lawsuit. But every four years, the Democratic Party tells women that they are being paid less because of their gender. They rally women and tell them, "If you don't vote for us, you will never have equality. You will always be oppressed." All kinds of statistics are tossed around. "Women earn seventy-two cents for every dollar a man makes" is the most common.

Are women really getting paid less for the same work? Absolutely not! Anyone can manipulate numbers to show what they want. The Democratic Party has made a living on false statistics and polls for many years. Ironically, many companies are now paying *women* more than men for the exact same work, in the name of "equality and attracting talent." I will document that hypocrisy shortly.

First, let's see how easy it is to manipulate numbers. One trick the Democrats use is to compare part-time working women to full-time working men. Of course, the man is making more; he's working more hours. But the Democrats leave that point out.

Another is to compare women who are younger and less experienced with older, more experienced men. You could easily do this in reverse. If you took a twenty-two-year-old male employed as an Army lieutenant, then compared him to a forty-year-old woman who is an Army colonel, she will be making double his pay.

But the Democrats never use women who are making more than men. That goes against gynocentrism; only the woman can be the victim. If a man earns more than a woman, it is discrimination. If a woman earns more than a man, it is "progress."

There are female doctors, lawyers, accountants, engineers, etc., who are earning more than their male counterparts. Why isn't that an issue with the feminists and gynocentrists? If they really strive for "equality," wouldn't women getting paid more be just as offensive? No, you have to continue the propaganda to incite hatred and get votes. Without angry women, the Democratic Party can't win a single election.

Here's a study that the Democrats will never acknowledge. In an article featured in *Time's* Business section titled *Workplace Salaries: At Last, Women on Top*, Belinda Luscombe gloats, "…the ship may finally be turning around: according to a new analysis of 2,000 communities by a market research company, in 147 out of 150 of the biggest cities in the U.S., the median full-time salaries of young women are 8% higher than those of the guys in their peer group."

In almost every major city, young women are earning almost 10 percent more than young men. Why don't the Democrats take that data into consideration? No, they hide this data and any other data that exposes their propaganda campaign.

As stated above, there isn't a single company in the United States that pays men more based on their gender (at least not openly). However, there are many companies that openly pay women more based on *their* gender. The excuse is, "We have to pay them more because there is a shortage of women in this field." But if that were true, male nurses would be paid more than female nurses, because there is a shortage of male nurses. There isn't a single hospital in the United States that pays male nurses more.

If the intention of paying women more is because there is a shortage of them, then you would pay men more in fields where there is a shortage of men. But that never happens! Only women can have special rights and incentives.

Do you see how pervasive gynocentrism truly is? It creeps into every area of life. If any company paid a man more because of his gender, they immediately get sued. But if a company pays women more based on their gender, they are applauded for furthering the advancement of women.

Let's take a look at some of the occupations that openly pay women more than men: aircraft mechanic, medical scientists, occupational therapy, dietician and nutritionist, respiratory therapy, operations research analyst, stockbroker, police detective, modeling, sales and marketing analyst, systems engineer, mechanical engineer, computer support specialist, technical fields like Social and Health Science, accounting clerks, and many other occupations. This translates into millions of high-paying jobs that woman earn more than men. Where is the outrage at this inequality? In reality, these numbers are swept under the rug by Democrats and gynocentrists.

Statistics are manipulated and data is hidden, all to deceive women and fill them with anger. This translates into votes. It has worked for many years, and the Party of Hate will be using it for years to come.

Here is one point that no gynocentrist or Democrat can hide from. In the last thirty years, the Democrats have had complete control of Washington, D.C. multiple times (the Presidency, the Senate, and the Congress, all at the same time). If they had complete political control of the country, why didn't they fix the "unequal pay" of women? They could have levied heavy fines on any company caught discriminating. But they didn't do a single thing. Why? Because there is no pay-gap for men and women doing the same work. Each election, the Democrats use the imaginary pay-gap to harvest votes. And, unfortunately, it works every time.

Chapter 6: College Admissions

Even though females comprise the majority of college students, they are considered a "minority" for scholarship and financial aid purposes. According to *The New York Times*, females account for 58 percent of the college population. For over thirty years, women have been the majority on college campuses. Only in America can the majority become the minority when it serves the purpose of political advantage. The Democratic Party isn't going to worry about facts and reality. There are votes to get. In the dirty deal between gynocentrists and the Democratic Party, they both got what they wanted. The Democrats got votes, and the gynocentrists got to stack the deck in favor of women.

If gynocentrism is going to rule supreme, then the majority of college educations need to go to women. They will become the future politicians, doctors, lawyers, CEO's, judges, and every other position of power. Women will climb to the top of every field, because they will outnumber men in every profession. Women will reign supreme.

Can you see the common thread again? Women don't have to fight or earn their way into a college program. They need special consideration because even tests are biased. **Absolute power through victimization, over and over!** A female raised in a wealthy family with average grades, will often get more assistance than a brilliant male who grew up in poverty.

The feminists and gynocentrists carry their "victim card" everywhere they go, like a shopper with an American Express card. It is an excuse for mediocrity. "Oh, if men weren't holding me back I could…" is the thought process hammered into impressionable young women, over and over, starting at an early age. Ironically, many women even complain about this bias, but they are shut out of the mainstream media.

Consider this quote from a woman named Janice Shaw Crouse, written in *The American Thinker*: "After forty years of preferential treatment in schools and the job market, many women are now better-educated and make more money than men." What? Why isn't this woman ever invited to speak at the Democratic Party National Convention? Because any woman who speaks the truth is considered a "traitor" to gynocentrism and the Democrats, that's why. She is supposed to fill women with anger, not give the true statistics.

Crouse goes on to lament, "Many women are finding it difficult if not impossible to find a husband who is their financial, career, or social equal." If women are now having trouble finding their equal, then that means there are more educated, high earning women than men. So how can women still be considered the underdog when applying for college?

As you have seen over and over in this book, the real numbers are hidden to further the "War on Women" propaganda. Truth is the enemy of the Democrats, which is why they control the media with an iron hand. If the people ever get the truth, they are out of power. This is why any opposing viewpoint is quickly shouted down and mocked by the mainstream media. March in lockstep with the script they hand you, or your career is finished.

There is another reason the Democrats and gynocentrists want the majority of college educations going to women. It is their laboratory of social engineering, where impressionable young women are quickly indoctrinated into hate and anger. Here is one example of the propaganda campaigns that are rampant on college campuses across America.

Take Back the Night Marches. These "marches" have been active on college campuses for decades. Young women are told that, "At least one out of every three women worldwide has been beaten, forced into sex, or otherwise abused in her lifetime by a partner, relative, friend, stranger, employer, and/or colleague."

Can you believe the vast, sweeping allegation? That at least a full 33 percent of women are abused? That translates into millions upon millions of young college students falling victim in some way. Colleges receive millions of dollars to "Raise awareness and prevent sex crimes on campus." Take Back the Night also sells T-shirts, wristbands, and other items. But if you ask where all this money goes, you will quickly be accused of "hate" and being "anti-women."

Many women's groups are disgusted with the propaganda young college students are bombarded with, and they are fighting back. The Independent Women's Forum (IWF), was fed up with "Victimology Feminism" and began their own campaign called,

Take Back the Campus. The IWF called campus feminism a "kind of cult" and criticized the feminists' statistics as "myths." Even though this is an organization of women, just like Concerned Women for America, the left-wing feminists called them "anti-women." Can that be any more ridiculous? According to the gynocentrists/feminists, any woman's group that disagrees with them is "anti-women." Millions of women are against themselves? No, millions of women are fed up with money hungry leeches spreading hate for financial gain.

Remember, it is only the left-wing rape industry that gets the government money. The women challenging them get no federal assistance. Peculiar, don't you think? When women say there is no rape epidemic on campus, they get nothing. But when liberal women's groups keep inflating rape on campus numbers, they get even more money. Why is that? As previously mentioned, the Democratic Party has a business deal with gynocentrists/feminists, and it goes like this: "Deliver us votes, and we will give you everything you want." As the gynocentrists/feminists stir up more hate, the Democrats get votes, and then more money comes in the form of government grants. This is why the feminists quickly lash out at women who oppose them (it costs them money). Furthermore, the Democrats get to rush in as the "savior" and grant more special rights to women's groups.

Let's revisit this quote from a previous chapter, "Men who are unjustly accused of rape can sometimes gain from the experience." Catherine Comins, Vassar College Assistant Dean of Student Life, as quoted in *Time Magazine*, June 3, 1991. Do you see how far back this mentality goes? How long they have poisoned our young women? The deeper you dig, the clearer the picture becomes. This isn't about leveling the playing field. This isn't about justice. It is about hate, money, and votes.

A woman named Heather MacDonald had the bad manners to publish an article called *The Campus Rape Myth* in *City Journal*. Ms. MacDonald stated the rape statistics are overblown, and does an excellent job of documenting the many groups making money out of the crisis. Of course, she was quickly ridiculed by the victim feminist culture. She won't be getting an invitation to speak at the Democratic Party National Convention, or any college campus.

With this information, it becomes clear why the Democrats and gynocentrists/feminists continue to manipulate college admissions. It is a twofold strategy. First, it ensures most of our future leaders will be women, as they will hold the majority of college degrees. Secondly, it gives easy access to manipulate women at an early age and harvest votes for the Democratic Party. So, when you hear the feminists screaming about equality, remember the true statistics you learned here. If they were truly concerned about equality, wouldn't they be infuriated that almost 60 percent of college admissions were going to one single gender?

No one is disputing these numbers. These are government statistics furnished by colleges and universities. For decades, women have represented the majority of college admissions. Each year, millions of bright young men get denied admission to prestigious colleges, while females with lower grades and SAT scores get accepted. These young men never discriminated against nor hurt anyone. But the hateful gynocentrists have no problem crushing their hopes and dreams. To the Democratic Party and gynocentrists, this is "equality."

Case Study: The Manipulation of Women
Brown vs. Warren

Brown vs. Warren is one of the most sickening cases of propaganda and media compliance in election history. When Senator Edward Kennedy died in 2009, it was just assumed a Democrat would walk into the senate seat with no difficulty. But an unknown Massachusetts State Senator, Scott Brown, appealed to the voters and won the seat. He seemed like an average citizen. He dressed casually and drove a pickup truck to campaign stops. This senate seat had been in the hands of Democrats for decades, and their blood was boiling. They handpicked a Harvard University Democratic Party insider for the dirty job that lay ahead. They needed to manipulate women and spread some hatred. Elizabeth Warren was the perfect candidate for the job.

Warren, worth approximately fifteen million dollars, became the poor, downtrodden symbol of female victimization. It was soon discovered that the multimillionaire Warren had claimed to be an American Indian in order to get her job at Harvard. Warren said she had high cheekbones, therefore, she must be American Indian. She further specified she was 1/32nd Native American.

How can anyone possibly state they are 1/32nd of any nationality? It is comical, to say the least. But the disgusting thing was Warren showed no remorse. That job was set aside for a minority, but the clearly Caucasian Warren wanted the job. So this multimillionaire claimed she was a "minority" to take it from those who truly deserved a chance.

To make things more repulsive, Warren's husband was already working for Harvard (no conflict of interest there, of course). So, this wealthy woman got a job that paid $400,000 per year for teaching one class a week. You read this correctly. She taught ONE class a week and was paid $400,000.

When the college was asked to provide data showing Warren was a Native American, they backed away and stated they "go by the description the employee gives," even though they reported they had a Native American female in their senior law professor ranks for years. Warren also refused to meet with Indian leaders to explain her heritage claims. If she had nothing to hide and was really a Native American, wouldn't she be proud to meet "her people?"

Warren's wealth and repeated deceitfulness started to bring her down in the polls, and she was trailing badly. It was time to play the hate card. Warren, with help from Vice President Joe Biden, suddenly declared there was a "War on Women." More specifically, Scott Brown was part of the War on Women. Suddenly, the attention was off her ill-earned millions and continued deceit.

Poor Elizabeth, she is a "victim" of a male war against her. The left-wing media gave her a free pass with this complete propaganda. This multimillionaire who took a job from a minority was now the victim. Not one network called her or Joe Biden out on this hate campaign. Scott Brown wasn't worth a fraction of Warren's wealth. He was as close to a working class senator as the country has ever seen, and he was the bad guy. She even played the gynocentric trump card and talked about rape comments in Missouri, thousands of miles away. What did that have to do with an election in Massachusetts?

Nothing, but it stirred the feminist hate base into action. Brown's wife and daughters spoke glowingly about him. He never said a negative word about women. None of that mattered. The Democrats wanted Kennedy's senate seat back, and they would do anything to get it.

They continued to call Brown *anti-women*, and a major player in the "War on Women" campaign. The hate strategy worked, and Brown continued to drop in the polls. Ironically, the only person who suffered in this imaginary war was Brown. The imaginary war delivered a senate seat to Elizabeth Warren.

Do you see the pattern over and over? Elizabeth Warren didn't have to earn a professor's job at Harvard. She just claimed she was a minority and walked right in. Warren didn't have to earn a senate seat. She just claimed she was a victim of a "War on Women" campaign and walked right in. This is evidence of **absolute power through victimization.** It has worked for the Democrats for decades, and they will continue to profit from hate.

Elizabeth Warren couldn't care less about the lives of ordinary women. She just manipulated them to get what she wanted. She is a multimillionaire who takes from others to further her goals.

When she finishes her six-year term in the senate, she will have done nothing about the "War on Women," because she knows there isn't one. Since the election ended, not one Democrat has even mentioned it. But when it comes time for the next election, suddenly the "War on Women" will be back in full force. The sheep will trot along to the voting booth and put her back in office.

Fifteen million dollars isn't enough for Elizabeth Warren. Open your pocketbooks, ladies. She needs more of *your* money. The real "war" is against the working people, people who don't receive $400,000 a year working a few hours per week. But, if they keep you distracted, you just might forget about that fact.

Chapter 7: The American Justice System: Inequality in Law and Punishment

According to The Huffington Post, men get longer prison sentences for the exact same crime. A study by Sonja Starr, an assistant law professor, found that *men are given much higher sentences than women convicted of the same crimes in federal court. The study found that men receive sentences that are 63 percent higher, on average, than their female counterparts. Starr also found that females arrested for a crime are also significantly more likely to avoid charges and convictions entirely, and are twice as likely to avoid going to jail at all, even when convicted.* Gynocentrism is so pervasive that it has completely infiltrated the civil and criminal courts.

If you skipped a few chapters, here is the Brian Banks case again. This one nails the current demise of justice so well that it deserves a repeat. In 2002, high school football star Brian Banks had a promising future. He had agreed to play football for the University of Southern California and was considered a potential professional football player. Then, classmate Wanetta Gibson claimed he dragged her into a stairwell and raped her. On her testimony, he was sent to prison for five years. Gibson received over one million dollars in a settlement from the school district, claiming it was "unsafe." After Banks was released from prison, Gibson contacted him on Facebook, met with him, and apologized for fabricating the story that ruined his life. Banks secretly recorded Gibson's confession. His conviction was overturned, but no charges were ever filed against Wanetta Gibson.

She spent over a million dollars from the legal settlement, living in luxury, while Banks sat in a prison for something he didn't do. Even with a taped confession from Gibson, she was never charged with anything. It gets even better. Gibson blew through the money and ended up on welfare, with two kids from different fathers. She was actually ordered to pay child support but then got out of that because she didn't have a job. Men go to prison for failure to pay child support, whether they have a job or not. However, the state has decided not to prosecute her for either lying about rape or failure to pay child support. No double-standard there?

If a man sent a woman to prison, was later caught on tape admitting that he committed perjury to send her there, and had filed false reports to do it, that man would be arrested immediately. But Gibson is still walking free. How did the system get this perverted? Is it just legal chaos and incompetence causing these kinds of discrepancies in the way justice is administered? No, it isn't chaos or incompetence. As I have proved, and will continue to prove, the Democratic Party has fought for years to create a special class of "rights" and even "immunity" for women. Even when women file false charges against men, they are immune from prosecution. They want women to know it is okay to falsely accuse men of sexual harassment or rape.

There are so many examples of this anti-male bias in the courts that it's difficult to pick and choose cases. Divorce court bias will be featured in a separate chapter. As stated previously, gynocentrism is deadly. Some women use abuse as an excuse to actually kill their husband. In many cases, the women stood to profit heftily from the deceased husband's death, and still get off without jail time.

Barbara Sheehan shot and killed her husband of seventeen years. She never called 911. She shot him eleven times as he shaved in the bathroom. How was she in imminent danger as he shaved? She played the "abuse" card and was found not guilty of murder.

The defense used the "Battered Women's Syndrome" card. Courts don't recognize any "Battered Men's Syndrome," even if a man is beaten daily by an abusive spouse. The bottom line is that he can't play that card. Only women can be the victim. In a bizarre conclusion, they found her guilty of a firearm's charge, and she spent several years in jail. With the system, it was okay that she had killed her husband. But, possessing a gun? Now that deserves to be punished!

If you think this is an isolated incident, how about the Mary Winkler story? This Tennessee woman fatally shot her preacher husband in the back. According to police after her arrest, Winkler said she didn't recall pulling the trigger. Then she said she apologized and wiped the blood that bubbled from her dying husband's lips as he asked, "Why?"

Of course, the defense claimed, "She was depressed and showed classic symptoms of Post-Traumatic Stress Disorder" (as covered on CNN). You guessed it, Mary Winkler was set free. She shoots her defenseless husband in the back, claims abuse, and gets to live her life as a free woman.

Can you name any case in history where a man shot his wife in the back, claimed abuse, and was set free? No, you can't. It has never happened. But women get away with this sort of revenge killing in all kinds of situations.

Women choose when life begins and when life ends. "He abused me, therefore, he needs to die." Make no mistake; gynocentrism is a female-worshipping religion.

The government passes the **Violence Against Women Act**, but of course, it never passes a **Violence Against Men Act**, even though they suffer from violence more than women. The courts recognize **Battered Women's Syndrome**, but don't recognize **Battered Men's Syndrome**. Surely, you are seeing the pattern over and over.

What if a man killed his wife, never called 911, and then he said she was abusive. Do you think he would be set free? Of course not. He would get life in prison. Even if the woman was known to be extremely violent, he would not be allowed to claim abuse.

The theory would go something like this: "He should have just walked out of the house and left her." But women don't have to do the logical and legal thing.

Only women can use the abuse card, courtesy of the Democrats. Both of these men were in defenseless positions when they were shot. But the women "felt" they were in danger. That's good enough to kill. Abuse is now the Holy Grail of victim feminists. It is a "Get out of jail-free card."

How about school teachers? Another study found that female sex-offenders get off much easier than men. Teachers sometimes get stupid and cross the line with students. It can be sexual texts, propositioning, or actual sexual contact.

Not so long ago, it seemed only men were this foolish. Male teachers have always received harsh sentences for sex with a minor. (There is the occasional aberration where the sentence is minor, but this is rare.)

In the last ten years, it seems the majority of these types of cases are now female teachers having sex with minor boys. In a strange deviation from the norm, feminists did a study called *Sex-Based Sentencing: Sentencing Discrepancies Between Male and Female Sex Offenders* published in *Feminist Criminology*.

The feminists actually thought they could prove women got harsher sentences. However, the researchers concluded: *"When all variables, sex, sentence length, and offense category were considered, a significant difference was recognized in sentence length, and **sentence length for men was longer, indicating a harsher penalty for the same or similar offense**. In no instance were women sentenced to longer or more severe sentences with regard to any sex offense."*

The fact feminists actually published these results is amazing. It completely contradicted what they had set out to prove. You have to wonder if they were gloating about this, which would indicate another example of the biased legal system that caters to women.

Furthermore, this study and others state that the number of sex offenses committed by women is underreported. So, determining the real number of female sex offenders is nearly impossible, although it is likely far less than men. But does this justify giving probation or less jail time for the same exact crime?

The Bureau of Justice Statistics found that killing a female, as opposed to a man, increased sentences by over 40 percent. So, killing a woman is even considered worse than killing a man? Gynocentrism is running rampant in the legal system.

Here is one last case that is a glaring example of the bias against men. It is considered the "Crown Jewel" of victim feminism. The case is older, but it showcases two very important points. One, it shows how long this has been going on. Two, it exposes the intensity of feminist/gynocentric hatred.

In 1993, Lorena Bobbitt cut her husband's penis off with a knife. She then took the severed penis and threw it in a field. When she was arrested shortly after, she told the police, "He always has an orgasm, and he doesn't wait for me to have an orgasm," the Ecuadorian-born Lorena complained. "He's selfish."

However, once the lawyers got involved, suddenly her story changed to, "He raped me."

Of course, she was found not guilty and never spent a day in prison. She was "depressed" and had "Post Traumatic Stress Disorder," just like the other women who killed or assaulted their husbands.

Both Lorena and her husband, John, were known to be abusive. But it only mattered that *he* was abusive. Her abusiveness was, of course, his fault. When a man is abusive, he is a monster. When a woman is abusive, she is merely reacting to some male oppression, and therefore, it isn't really her fault. Her abusiveness and violence were *his* fault. Lorena Bobbitt was later arrested for assaulting her own mother. What was the excuse then?

This case brought out the most notorious display of feminist hatred all across America. Feminist groups celebrated the severing of a man's penis. They didn't know the facts of the case or anything about Lorena Bobbitt's history. But, the feminists turned her into a national hero for doing what they all dreamed of—cutting off a man's penis.

Lorena Bobbitt was then featured on the cover of *Vanity Fair*, in a bathing suit, posing innocently. The magazine stated she had become a **national folk heroine.** Sympathetic women were quoted throughout the magazine, relieved that the "monster" got what he deserved. However, the media rarely mentioned that her initial complaint was "…he doesn't wait for me to orgasm." They just jumped right on the rape bandwagon. Even the jury found John Bobbitt not guilty of rape.

Imagine if a man mutilated his wife's vagina with a knife, and then told police she didn't satisfy him. But when the lawyer got involved, he suddenly changed his story to, "She was abusive." Do you think the courts would allow him to claim "depression" and "Post Traumatic Stress Disorder" in his defense? Not a chance.

The judge would probably reprimand his defense lawyer for even daring to try. He would be sentenced to many years in prison. Now imagine the man actually did get off and was featured on the cover of Sports Illustrated as a "Hero." Feminists would be marching across America, the Justice Department would be reopening the case, and Sports Illustrated would probably be fined millions by the government. But when a woman does it, it is okay. Only women can be the victim. This is the Democratic Party's version of "equality."

Case Study: Birth Control

Even in the medical field, gynocentrism is taking control. This case study is only one example of this. The following chapter will further this argument quite well, but, let's continue.

Feminists/gynocentrists have long argued that government can't tell them what to do with their body. What they choose to do with their own body is a "privacy issue." A feminist slogan is, "Stay out of my vagina!" and this phrase has become quite popular with the Democrats (a classy bunch, indeed). However, it wasn't long until feminists demanded that government and corporations subsidize "their vagina" when it was convenient for them.

In congressional hearings, Sandra Fluke testified that women were suffering because religious employers weren't paying for their birth control. She stated that women were approaching her daily with tales of incredible hardship all because someone else wouldn't pay for their contraceptives. These women are "suffering medically, emotionally, and financially."

The Democrats staged this whole interview to justify making employers pay for *women's* birth control, even if it was against their religion. This was to round up the feminist vote. Notice there was no mention of birth control for men. Can you imagine if The Affordable Care Act only covered men's birth control? It is almost impossible to imagine. The mainstream media would be "outraged" by this incredible sexist discrimination. Not one news outlet has mentioned that men get no coverage. No bias there?

The feminist stance goes something like this, "It's my body. How dare you question me? Stay out of my vagina. Pay for my birth control and shut your mouth. If I get pregnant, your insurance premiums will pay for my abortion. You can pay for my vagina when I say so, and that is all you can do."

Because feminists want birth control, it is now a constitutional right. But the right does not extend to men. With gynocentrism, the man cannot have equal rights, even with birth control. But, the Democrats didn't stop there. They needed to show that gynocentrism overpowers all. The Constitution guarantees Americans the right of Religious Freedom without government interference. The pilgrims fled England for this very reason—freedom of religion.

Even if an employer has deep religious beliefs, as many do, they lose their constitutional rights; they must pay for the contraceptives! The Democrats needed to show that gynocentrism overpowers people's religion, overpowers the Constitution, and reigns supreme. **Bow at their altar, not yours**.

Chapter 8: Disease and Gynocentrism

The Democratic Party will use anything to divide and manipulate people. Disease is no exception. There is a hierarchy even amongst the sick.

Not so long ago, AIDS was the "Holy" disease of the left wing. People with AIDS were referred to as "heroes." If you got diabetes, you were just an unlucky statistic. The Democrats got whatever mileage they could out of AIDS, but something was missing. For one thing, AIDS infected mostly gay men. As a percentage of the population, their numbers were small. There just wasn't enough bang for the Democratic buck. They needed a new disease, something that appealed to a majority of the population. Then, it came to them. Breast cancer was perfect! The majority of the population is female, and the feminists love anything that favors women.

According to The World Health Organization, there are 14,199 diseases known to mankind. But suddenly, all you hear about is breast cancer. Heart disease kills fifteen times as many people as breast cancer. Lung cancer kills ten times as many people per year. But, all you see are pink ribbons everywhere you look—ATM machines, bumper stickers, billboards, radio commercials, television commercials, on and on. There are marches all around America to "raise awareness" and collect money. There is a silent theme, "There is no disease but breast cancer. All others are insignificant." A new gynocentric religion was born. Instead of a Star of David or Crucifix, there is now the pink ribbon.

Breast cancer is nowhere near the top killer in the United States. So then, what's all this intensity about? Simply put, the Democrats and gynocentrists jumped right on the vulnerability bandwagon and helped create another victim industry. They exploit the real fear of women for money and political gain. It fits their agenda like a glove.

The disease is virtually exclusive to women. It is a perfect symbol for the new America, women first! "You better vote for us. We are the only ones who care. Give as much money as you can."

Who will dare to speak out against this manipulation of disease and funding? If you open your mouth, you are "anti-women." Prostate cancer kills almost as many men as breast cancer kills women (30,000 vs. 40,000, respectively.) But, if you mention this fact to feminists, be prepared for a hate-filled verbal lashing. "How dare you even mention prostate cancer? That kills men. Who cares?" Men often donate money and walk in marches to help fight breast cancer. Have you ever seen a single march that focuses on raising money for prostate cancer?

As usual, if you follow the money trail, there are people who are becoming wealthy off of women's illness. If you think this is extreme, consider the following points. Nancy Brinker, founder of Susan G. Komen, has made millions "helping women" prevent and treat breast cancer. Her latest salary was $684,000 per year. She also billed the charity $133,507.00 for "expenses" between 2007 and 2009. She even earns more than The American Red Cross CEO, which is ten times bigger. This is the gynocentric mindset. Even though the Red Cross is bigger and helps more people in many situations, she's fighting breast cancer! That's more important; therefore, she deserves to be paid more. She is also known to live a lavish lifestyle.

In a report featured in *The Daily Beast*, former Komen employees refer to Nancy Brinker as follows, "An imposing figure who flies first-class, prefers five-star hotels, and generally exhibits an entitled air. Employees don't call her "Nancy," said the sources. They are expected to call her "Ambassador Brinker."

Jezebel added this in their own story, "Brinker doesn't need the money, as she made out like a bandit in her 2003 divorce from millionaire Norman Brinker. She jets between her home in the Ritz Carlton in Washington, D.C. and her second home in Palm Beach, Florida."

Sound familiar? Multimillionaire Elizabeth Warren takes a job from a minority, because she wanted it, not needed it. Nancy Brinker takes millions in pay from Komen, not because she needed any of it, but because she wanted even more money. This is the gynocentric way: *It's all about me.*

With all the money Brinker has taken and spent, thousands of women could have had mammograms and treatments. Thousands! But if you bring this up, you are "anti-women."

As previously stated, someone is usually getting rich off of other peoples' miseries. Breast cancer is now an industry. When people donate, they do it to help a woman in need. They don't do it to support Nancy Brinker's lavish lifestyle.

Then again, most Democrats are millionaires. But they are for "the working people." Just like Brinker, they get wealthier exploiting people's frustrations and even their illnesses. If you doubt a connection between the breast cancer movement and the Democrats, or a connection with the feminists, here it is on a silver platter. Komen announced they would no longer give money to Planned Parenthood, a major component of the Democratic Party. The backlash almost destroyed Komen and their fundraising dropped sharply.

Why would all this happen? Because the left-wing, Democrat-controlled media went on a crusade against Komen and fired up all the feminists. Komen was "anti-women." They weren't shelling out money to the loyal troops anymore. Komen quickly backed off and continued to fund Planned Parenthood. Bottom line: the Democratic Party would destroy them if they didn't.

Democratic representative, Marty Walz, helped Planned Parenthood get buffer-zone laws passed. What was the payback? Walz was recently hired by Planned Parenthood, making $250,000 per year! All of these organizations that manipulate women are under the control of the Democrats.

Furthermore, the cult-like mentality that the breast cancer industry spreads is harmful. It says one sick person is more important than the next. Hearing, "Mom has breast cancer" is terrifying to any family. But so is, "Dad had a heart attack," or "Little Joey has leukemia." If a woman has a stroke, is that less important than breast cancer?

Many feminists actually believe some diseases are more important than others, particularly if it affects mostly women. During Breast Cancer Awareness Month, all the men of the National Football League wear pink shoes or bracelets to show their "sensitivity." Have you ever seen any female athlete raising awareness for prostate cancer? No, you haven't. Only women can be the victim!

The shameless profiting that goes on is also pathetic. An e-mail from a local car dealer asked people to help them "raise awareness" of breast cancer. "Awareness" is everywhere, who doesn't know about breast cancer. The car dealer was looking to sell cars and using breast cancer to get people into the showroom.

A furniture dealer advertised on the radio, "Buy some furniture, and help fight breast cancer." They are using breast cancer to sell furniture! That was their primary goal. If they were really looking to help someone, they would donate money themselves, not ask you to donate when you buy from them and purchase a kitchen set.

This chapter is not to mock or belittle breast cancer. It kills women and hurts their loved ones. Efforts to help prevent and treat are admirable. It is the exploiting of the disease for political and financial gain that is reprehensible.

No disease is any fun to have. The Democrats and gynocentrists need to stop the divide-and-conquer politics they have played for years. Stop exploiting women! Stop manipulating them for votes and money. If the Democrats really cared more about women than other people do, and if there really was a War on Women, then maybe John Kerry, Joe Biden, Nancy Pelosi, Bill Clinton, et al. would give some of *their* millions to help out. Don't hold your breath waiting.

Chapter 9: Gynocentrism and the Self-Esteem Movement

Somewhere along the line, the "experts" determined that raising people's self-esteem would solve all our problems. The only reason people did bad things, and the only reason people committed crimes, was due to them having low self-esteem. When children fail a test, certainly their low self-esteem is to blame.

In the decades that have passed since this "epiphany" hit main street America, there has been heated debate. Many educators and sociologists feel this whole self-esteem crusade has actually hurt our children. But that didn't stop the gynocentrists from hijacking this movement as well. Self-esteem programs can only target girls. Making boys feel better about their gender is a threat to females and unacceptable.

According to author Janice Shaw Crouse, "We've spent forty years pushing girls ahead and holding boys back." And she further states, "The Pew study notes that women are leaving school better-prepared for today's job market, but the 'same ole-same ole' educational priorities reign, and our boys are still getting a raw deal in school."

Her article exposes the true mission of self-esteem programs— bring boys down, bring girls up. Gynocentrism has even infiltrated social programs targeting people's very self-worth. If the feminist/gynocentric/inner goddess movement is to dominate American society, then boys need to be pushed down the ladder to second-class citizens.

How females feel about themselves is critically important. They must be showered with praise, told they are smart, amazing, and can accomplish anything. They are told to celebrate their unique qualities as a girl. These types of programs are weaved into the school systems and institutions across America.

There is **Women's History Month,** which highlights the contributions of women to events in history and contemporary society. However, there isn't a single program in any school or social institution that "celebrates" being male. There is no **Men's History Month.** This would be a threat to the female self-esteem. Anything that men accomplished was under the dark cloud of oppression.

To the feminists, any attempt to make boys feel better about their gender is sexism. Making girls feel better about their gender is "progress." It is viewed as "leveling the playing field." Millions of teenaged boys, who never discriminated against anyone, are brushed aside by a feminist-dominated educational system. Many of these boys come from poverty, broken homes, dysfunctional homes, and are at risk. As far as self-esteem goes, these boys don't have much hope for their future. But the feminists couldn't care less. Let them all crash and burn, because that leaves more opportunity for girls.

If you have trouble believing some teachers literally hate boys, think of the previous chapter on sexual harassment. A six-year-old boy kissed a girl's hand, and the female principal suspended him for sexual harassment. That is pure hatred. To put it in perspective, imagine a six-year-old girl kissing a boy's hand, and then the male principal labels her as a sex offender. He would probably lose his job for shattering her fragile self-esteem.

Of course, there are millions in grants to improve girl's self-esteem. (Notice how money is always a factor with feminists.) There was a $300,000 grant from Verizon to "Help teenage girls build self-esteem and avoid violent relationships" in the Los Angeles area. Why can't they also help at-risk boys in that same area?

Los Angeles has a high crime rate and many boys join gangs. Why are they unimportant? The Dr. Phil Foundation made a grant to **The Awesome Girls Mentoring Program.** Why was there no grant for *The Awesome Boys Mentoring Program*? That's because there is no Awesome Boys Mentoring Program. If someone started a program just for boys, they would immediately be accused of discrimination and boycotted. Lawsuits would likely follow. There would be "shock" in the mainstream media, and a definite outrage that girls were being excluded. But when girls are the only beneficiary, it's okay. We need to improve their self-esteem.

Do you see how gynocentrism has made one-sided discrimination the law of the land? This wasn't accidental. The feminists worked for decades to do this. All their visions for a female-centered America are coming to fruition.

Even Dove Soap has started their own *girl's* self-esteem movement. In their words, "Dove® is committed to building positive self-esteem and inspiring all women and girls to reach their full potential. All October, we are celebrating unstoppable girls. Join the conversation to support positive self-esteem." They celebrate unstoppable girls; there is no celebration for unstoppable boys. If Dove had a campaign just for boys, there would be a tremendous backlash.

These girls-only programs are everywhere, including government-funded programs. Recently, in New York City, Mayor Bloomberg, Deputy Mayor Gibbs and Women's Commission Executive Director Davis launched New York City Girls' Self-Esteem Project. Sorry, no boy's project. It goes against gynocentrism.

The state of Maine is "Investing in the power of women and the dreams of girls." Here is their statement: "The Maine Women's Fund is a public foundation, creating lasting change by investing in the power of women and the dreams of girls. We are passionate in our belief that when women and girls thrive, communities prosper. The Maine Women's Fund builds economic security for Maine women and girls and strengthens communities through grants to non-profit organizations and the advancement of women's philanthropic leadership."

This is taxpayers' money that is being used exclusively to help females, and it is blatant discrimination and illegal. All the state and federal grants exclude males. Can you imagine if there were programs all across America aimed at helping boys, only boys, and females were excluded? If millions of tax dollars were being used to only help boys, then programs would be shut down instantly by the courts and deemed as unconstitutional. It would be a violation of "Equal Protection." The politicians who approved such a thing would be called bigots and sexists, and they would be voted out of office. But when it only benefits females, then it's okay. If you say a word against it, you are "anti-women."

This madness sweeping across America is like some dystopian George Orwell novel. The place the government tortures people is known as "The Ministry of Love." The place where the government spreads lies is known as "The Ministry of Truth." And even though women have every advantage over men, they are officially recognized as the underdog victim.

The self-esteem movement isn't just a touchy, feel good effort. There is a very sinister side to it, and a deliberate effort that seeks to knock males down.

In her bestselling book, *The War Against Boys: How Misguided Feminism Is Harming Our Young Men,* author Christina Hoff Sommers tears the feminist propaganda machine apart. She states, "Our young men are greatly at risk, yet the best-known studies and experts insist that it's girls who are in need of our attention. The highly publicized "girl crisis" has led to many changes in American schools, politics, and parenting...but at what cost?"

Christina Hoff Sommers argues that, "Our society has continued to overemphasize the troubles of girls while our boys suffer from the same self-esteem and academic problems. Boys need help, but not the sort of help they've been getting." She won't be speaking at the Democratic Party National Convention. She is a "traitor" to gynocentrism. If you want to know what is really happening in our schools, and learn how "studies" are manipulated by the feminists, Sommer's book is highly recommended.

In the last few decades, there has been an incredible spike in female valedictorians. Most studies indicate that over 70 percent of valedictorians are female. In a relatively short period of time, a few decades, there was a complete reversal in academic performance.

Do you think that boys suddenly became less intelligent? Or do you believe teachers are inflating girls' grades to help their "self-esteem?" If you think this is unlikely, you need to look into our school systems. Many teachers complain they are being pressured to inflate grades. Considering most of our teachers were indoctrinated by feminists on college campuses, whose grades are they inflating the most?

There is concrete evidence to prove this theory. Many authors are writing books on this subject (Hannah Rosin's *The End of Men and the Rise of Women,* et al.).

Here is a quote from one study published in the *Journal of Human Resources*, in conjunction with a major university: "Teachers tend to assess students on non-cognitive, socio-emotional skills. This has had a significant impact on boys' later achievement because, while objective test scores are important, it is teacher-assigned grades that determine a child's future with class placement, high school graduation, and college admissibility. Eliminating the factor of non-cognitive skills…almost eliminates the estimated gender gap in reading grades, Cornwell found. He said he found it surprising that although boys out-perform girls on math and science test scores, girls out-perform boys on teacher-assigned grades…"

Take note of that last sentence, "Girls out-perform boys **on teacher-assigned grades**." Feminist teachers are actually practicing their own version of Affirmative Action. Extra credit is given to girls for being "more involved" and having better "participation," thus slanting grade point average in their favor.

Boys are also sent to Special Education classes by the female teachers twice as often as girls. According to Jennifer J. Haggerty, *University of Missouri at Kansas City, School of Law,* "Gender Disparity: Boys v. Girls in Special Education discusses why boys outnumber girls in special education classes in a ratio of 2:1. Gender disparity in special education is a severe problem which is increasing as there are relatively few male educators. Male educators are needed in the educational system to counteract female teachers' tendencies to send male students to special education based upon behavioral characteristics, not upon educational disabilities."

Boys who don't fit in with the feminist teaching agenda can be sent to special education and stigmatized for life. If male teachers were sending girls into special education at twice the rate of boys, there would be a national investigation by the federal government. The teachers would be fired. But when boys get a bad deal, it is business as usual. The self-esteem movement gives feminist teachers a license to hate. They have to give the girls better grades, because it is important to their "self-esteem." This is why the Democrats and gynocentrists ambushed the movement as quickly as possible. Once again, it's **power through victimization**.

Case Study: SBA Loans

Many people dream of starting a small business. They want to break free from the rat race and build a better future for themselves. Thanks to the gynocentrists, women's dreams are more important than men's. If you are a man, you are essentially on your own. Unfortunately, there is no special program for you. It's you against the world. If you are a woman, it is an entirely different story.

There are government programs that assist *only* women in starting a business and securing funding. This is why the number of female-owned businesses has exploded in the last ten years. Once again, women don't have to pay the price, but men do. The Democrats have created many programs to assist women, only women, in reaching their dreams.

A man can live in poverty, be a veteran who served his country, and still not qualify for any of the help women get. Imagine the insult to veterans? They serve their country for little money, perhaps fighting in a war and bearing the scars forever; then they have to watch their own government work against them.

Women who are financially well-off qualify for help, while disadvantaged men qualify for no government help. The Democrats refuse to recognize this as discrimination. The largest organization that helps women is The Small Business Administration. The government actually gives women-owned businesses preference in many government contracts.

Here is the SBA's definition of an "Economically Disadvantaged Women-Owned Small Business:"

"A woman is presumed economically disadvantaged if she has a personal net worth of less than $750,000, her adjusted gross yearly income averaged over the three years preceding the certification does not exceed $350,000, and the fair market value of all her assets (including her primary residence and the value of the business concern) does not exceed $6 million" (As listed on SBA.gov).

A woman is disadvantaged if her personal net worth is less than $750,000? She is disadvantaged if she earns $349,000 per year? She is disadvantaged if her net worth is $5,900,000?

Consider this: If a man is living out of a van with $20 to his name, he isn't considered "disadvantaged," and he has no privilege of even being considered for a special SBA program.

If you look into the SBA Veteran's programs, they essentially give lip service. Here is what they say: "The Office of Veterans Business Development's mission is to maximize the availability, applicability and usability of all administration small business programs for Veterans, Service-Disabled Veterans, Reserve Component Members, and their Dependents or Survivors."

Could they be anymore vague? Their mission is to "maximize the availability, applicability and usability" of programs. It is just typical government lip service with no actual programs for male veterans. But, here is what they do for **female** veterans. On the SBA webpage, they are the "Spotlight." (Of course, they need special attention, they're women.) Their promise and help is very specific:

"The Office of Veterans Business Development, U.S. Small Business Administration, is announcing the *Women Veterans Igniting the Spirit of Entrepreneurship–VWISE-2014-01* Cooperative Agreement for continuation of the National training program for **female** veterans, transitioning military *female* personnel, and spouses/companions of veterans currently operating small businesses. Organizations interested in submitting applications are to apply through the grants.gov web-portal. Only applications submitted through grants.gov will be considered; applications must be complete and include all the required forms. Incomplete applications will not be considered nor will those submitted by any means other than through grants.gov." After this statement, there are links to help women get started.

Male veterans need not apply for any of the above. There isn't one single program that aims to help only male veterans. This is taxpayer money being used to only help women. This is blatant discrimination and violates the equal protection clause of the United States. This money is set aside for women by written law; it is not a "suggestion" by the government. Are you finally seeing the sinister side of gynocentrism? Even when men serve their country, they are less important than women who serve their country. What is the justification for this one? Why would female veterans need special help over male veterans? The fact is, they don't.

According to the National Coalition for the Homeless, the U.S. Department of Veterans Affairs (VA) says the nation's homeless veterans are mostly males (4 percent are females). Ninety-six percent of homeless veterans are male! Two-hundred-thousand veterans are homeless, and even though only 4 percent are female, they still need extra help!

Do you see the pattern? The real numbers mean nothing. It doesn't matter who needs more help. Only women can be the victim! Even when women have a tremendous advantage, they get extra help. This is the Democratic Party and the gynocentrists at work. They will do anything to buy votes and stay in power. They will easily discriminate against the men who fought for the American people's freedom.

Chapter 10: Affirmative Action

Affirmative Action was never intended to help women. You read that correctly. It was never intended to help women. If you mention this to a Democrat or gynocentrist, be prepared for a hate-filled speech along with accusations of sexism and plenty of foul language.

Affirmative Action was intended to help Americans of African descent who were dragged here in chains and enslaved for hundreds of years. It was to be a *temporary measure* to level the playing field for African Americans. As usual, the Democrats and gynocentrists wasted no time hijacking this well-intentioned law. This shows the arrogance and indifference of the feminists, and also shows that the Democrats will sell out anybody for votes. To compare women who grew up in freedom with those who were dragged here in chains is an absolute outrage. Simply because women didn't have all the rights of men does not equal slavery, not even close!

Even though Affirmative Action was intended for the descendants of slaves, it is white women who are the greatest beneficiary of the program. It reminds me of multimillionaire Elizabeth Warren stealing the job from a minority. The feminists still voted for her because they agreed with her actions and thought the same way— *it's all about me!* She didn't need the job like many minorities desperately do. She wanted it and that is all that mattered. It furthered *her* agenda and goals.

The feminists and gynocentrists felt the same way about Affirmative Action. It didn't matter who needed it the most. It could help *them* get what *they* wanted, and that is the most important thing. They had no trouble dismissing the past of African Americans, a past of slavery and little opportunity when slavery ended. In the gynocentric mind, they are always the biggest victim. Being a woman was worse than slavery. So they quickly hijacked the program and reaped the greatest benefits from it. The Democrats saw votes in the making and were willing accomplices in this theft of opportunity.

In an article titled "Affirmative Action: Who Was it Really Meant For?" author Alexis Gigi Thornton echoes a similar complaint. She states, "Which group of people was Affirmative Action created for? Yeeesss, you can say it—*Black People* or Black Americans to be more specific. From the outset, Affirmative Action was envisioned as a temporary remedy or measure that was supposed to end once there was a 'level playing field' for **all** Americans."

She further states, "Our ancestors were victims of a historic national crime…our ancestors were dragged here in chains, shackled and sold on the auction block like cattle. So, one of the forms of reparations *IS* Affirmative Action."

And for anyone who isn't getting her point, she ends it plainly, "The original mission of Affirmative Action was to address **<u>ONLY ONE GROUP OF PEOPLE</u>** that has spent over four-hundred years enslaved (some books state two-hundred years, but that's incorrect)."

She is absolutely correct. The United States government created it to help only African Americans. And even though Ms. Thornton is an African American, she won't be getting an invitation to speak at the Democratic Party National Convention. She is speaking the truth and they hide from that. Besides, to the Democrats, whoever delivers the most votes gets the most help; not the ones who need help most.

The feminists have more political power, so they get the most help from Affirmative Action. Again, we see the evil nature of gynocentrism. They literally rip things out of people's hands because *they* want it, not need it. Even though the program was created for African Americans, white middle-class women have gained the most from it. This is the gynocentrist's version of "fairness."

There isn't even any economic consideration in the program. It blindly helps women from wealthy families over men who grow up in poverty. When it comes to Affirmative Action, a man can work harder, have better grades, and need the assistance, but get turned down because of his gender. On the flip side, a woman can come from a wealthy family, have poor grades, and still get the job before a man does.

In many banks and office places, you will see exclusively female staff. This is diversity? However, you will not walk into any decent-sized place of employment and see only male staff. They would be sued instantly.

Even traditionally male-dominated companies have been forced to diversify. Visit any Home Depot, and you will see as many female employees as male, even though hardware and construction have historically been dominated by men. The same is not true in reverse. Industries that have been traditionally dominated by females face no pressure to diversify. There's no program to recruit more male dental hygienists. There's no program aimed at recruiting more male teachers. They say there is a need, but there is no pressure on schools to "diversify." You only need to diversify when there are a lot of men in the company. If there are all women, that is progress.

To add insult to injury, there are more women in the workforce than men; they are the majority. But they are still considered the minority for Affirmative Action purposes and getting hired first. Just like college admissions, the majority is considered the minority, because it gets the Democrats' votes. The real numbers are hidden.

The Atlantic had this to say, "**The End of Men:** Earlier this year, women became the majority of the workforce for the first time in U.S. history. Most managers are now women too. And for every two men who get a college degree this year, three women will do the same. For years, women's progress has been cast as a struggle for equality. **But what if equality isn't the end point?** What if modern, postindustrial society is simply better suited to women?"

They ask, "But what if equality isn't the end point?" That is a rhetorical question, because they know the answer. Equality was never the endpoint! The gynocentric mission has always been to have a female-centered society. Power through victimization has brought their vision to fruition. If they really were concerned about equality, they would take note that most managers are now women and try to correct the imbalance, and then bring it to an even number of men and women. But they still say women need more promotions to "level the playing field." The playing field *is* uneven; it's in favor of women. So, why push for even more women? It's because the goal has always been to bring men down and to bring women up. Gynocentrism is rooted in hate, not logic, or real statistics.

One feminist website called *20-First* proudly proclaims, "The milestone has at last been cleared: More women than men were on payrolls in January 2010, according to US Labor Department statistics for the month."

At last, like they have waited patiently for women to have more power in the workforce. In an article titled, *Workplace Salaries: At Last, Women on Top*, featured in *Time's* Business section, Belinda Luscombe gloats, "...the ship may finally be turning around: according to a new analysis of 2,000 communities by a market research company, in 147 out of 150 of the biggest cities in the U.S., the median full-time salaries of young women are 8% higher than those of the guys in their peer group."

The *Economist* proudly put out this article. "**We did it! The rich world's quiet revolution: women are gradually taking over the workplace**. At a time when the world is short of causes for celebration, here is a candidate. Within the next few months, women will cross the 50 percent threshold and become the majority of the American workforce. Women already make up the majority of university graduates in the OECD countries and the majority of professional workers in several rich countries, including the United States.

Women run many of the world's great companies, from PepsiCo in America to Areva in France. The theme is the same in all three articles: Finally, we are taking control of everything. This is a cause for celebration! When men are the majority of anything, it is oppression. But when women are the majority, it is the way it should be. When men earn more, it is evil, however, when women earn more, it is the way it should be. Notice none of them mentioned the word "equality." That word only comes in to play when women aren't winning.

Furthermore, Affirmative Action is never need-based. It never rewards service or sacrifice. It blindly favors women over men. As stated previously, a wealthy female often gets preference over a better qualified male who came out of poverty. Not just in the job market, this is especially true in college admissions.

Even veterans face this reverse discrimination. When men serve their country, they earn "Veteran's Preference" for government jobs after discharge. However, Affirmative Action actually trumps Veteran's Preference in many cases. A woman who never served or sacrificed anything, will often get preference over a man who sacrificed greatly for his country. This is justice? This is leveling the playing field? No, it is simply a selfish power grab backed by hate and the Democratic Party. Discrimination is discrimination. Just because it "works for you" doesn't make it right.

Chapter 11: Gender Bias in Divorce Court

Even though gynocentrism is pervasive in American society, and the bias in favor of women is now the legal standard, the blatant sexism and bigotry of divorce courts is still astonishing. The divorce courts in every state simply "assume" that women are better parents. There is no rational or scientific data to back this assumption. This is the power of the gynocentrists and the Democratic Party working together.

The courts can systematically discriminate against one-half of the nation's population with no consequences. If men were getting custody of the children 70-80 percent of the time, there would be feminist marches across the country. We would witness shock and outrage by the left-wing media, with tearful interviews of women who had their children ripped away by the sexist courts.

Let's start from the beginning. The vast majority of divorces are initiated by women (70 percent). This is because women know they will get a much better deal than men. They will almost certainly get custody and extra income from child support. Therefore, far fewer men file for divorce; they know the system is going to favor the wife.

Even though some judges pretend to be "indignant" about these allegations, and "shocked" that someone would suggest women get extreme preference in every phase of divorce, the statistics expose these judges as liars. Numbers don't lie, but people certainly do. If there was no bias in divorce courts, then women wouldn't get sole custody 60 percent of the time while fathers get sole custody 15 percent of the time. (In 25 percent of the cases where joint custody is awarded, even then, the child usually lives with the mother, giving women physical custody 85 percent of the time). The system gives women sole custody four times more often than men. To say this just randomly happens is an insult to anyone who can think. It is statistically impossible that women get sole custody four times as often as men, year after year, without extreme bias.

There is something called "The Law of Large Numbers." It works something like this: If you flipped a coin 1,000 times, it will land on heads about 50 percent of the time, and tails about 50 percent of the time. This is because every time you flip a coin, random chance comes into play. That is why it eventually evens out. It has to, because you flipped the coin so many times. The same should hold true in divorce court.

There are millions of divorces each year in America. Each case has its own variables (adultery, financial problems, fighting, etc.). With this large of a volume, the final numbers should rest at about 50/50 with all things being equal. But, each and every year, women get custody in the overwhelming majority of cases. The judges can lie and deceive all they want. They have a clear agenda and bias towards women.

This bigotry against men has given rise to father's groups all across the country. Of course, these father's groups are shunned by the mainstream media. Only women can be the victim. It would make a compelling story or investigative series, but none of the mainstream media will touch the story. Why not? Because it doesn't fit with the "War on Women" propaganda that the media is expected to push on the public, that's why. Anything that says men are getting a bad deal must be swept under the rug. If they run this story about divorce court bias, the Democrats will come after them with a vengeance.

There are many women who speak out against this injustice. But, once again, the mainstream media has a virtual blackout against them. The internet is swarming with articles and blogs by people desperate for justice, by legal professionals who are disgusted with the criminal actions of divorce court judges, by fathers who committed no crime but haven't seen their children for years.

Dr. Tara J. Palmatier vents extreme frustration with the incredible bias against men in divorce court. She states, "If you're a man considering marriage, there are some statistics you should know *before* you go ring shopping. What many people don't know is that women initiate approximately 70% of all divorces. In my opinion, the primary reason women initiate divorces in 70% of divorce cases is because most women stand to gain far more than they have to lose if they choose to divorce.

This figure would probably be closer to 50% if men were able to leave dissatisfying and/or abusive marriages without the threat of being destroyed by the family court system and losing their assets and children just as most women are able to do when they initiate divorce. Not only do women initiate 70% of divorces, women are awarded primary custody in 82.6% of custody cases and this figure has remained largely unchanged since the 1994 U.S. Census." Even though men are often accused of abuse in divorce courts, Dr. Palmatier gives the real numbers, "What's more, 61% of all child abuse is committed by biological mothers (Department of Health and Human Services Report on Nationwide Child Abuse)."

She goes on with even more disturbing information most people don't know, such as, "What's more, the Bradley amendment ensures that even if a man can prove he is the victim of paternity fraud, that he cannot be absolved from paying child support to a child that is not his biological offspring, which brings us to another disturbing statistic. Approximately 30% of paternity tests submitted come back negative. That's nearly one-third of challenged paternity cases proving the woman lied."

This is surreal. A woman fools a man into paying child support. But when he finds out it was never his child, the law says HE STILL HAS TO PAY THE WOMAN WHO RUINED HIS LIFE! Can you imagine if the situation was reversed? This injustice would never be put onto a woman. No court would ever allow it.

Finally, she shows the blatant discrimination against men with this information, "What about brave men who marry a second time? Men can have their new spouse's income held against them and used to extort more child and spousal support to their ex-wives. For instance, in Massachusetts, judges frequently include a second spouse's income as part of "total household income" and use that figure to determine whether the payer, usually a man, has enough income to keep paying spousal support. However, if the ex-wife remarries, her new spouse is under no legal obligation to financially support his stepchildren. The court's rationale? Hey, they're not his children and, therefore, not his responsibility. Yet, it is the new wife's responsibility to give a portion of her salary to her husband's ex-wife and children. Can someone please explain the logic of this to me?"

Sorry, Dr. Palmatier, no one can explain the logic of this, because there is no logic involved. It is simply bias, hate, bigotry, and a system rigged by the Democratic Party to buy votes. We have become a gynocentric nation. In all matters of law, dispute, and gender relations, the woman must always receive preferential treatment.

Dr. Palmatier's observations don't tell the entire ugly story. It gets downright criminal in some cases. There is a reason divorced men commit suicide far more often than divorced women—it's because the system often destroys his life. A woman can simply make an allegation, with no proof, and the burden is on the man to "disprove it." If someone says you threatened them, how can you disprove it with no witnesses? You can't.

This is why women can get a restraining order against a man with only a few words. A man can be pulled out of his own home by nothing more than an allegation. However, it is almost impossible for a man to get a restraining order against a woman.

The *Journal of Family Violence,* an academic journal on domestic violence issues, published the following as part of a study. "*A Measure of Court Response to Requests for Protection, by the Fatherhood Coalition's Steve Basile, examined the 209A restraining orders issued in Gardner District Court in 1997. The study reveals a clear double standard in the court response to alleged victims of domestic abuse/violence. In each of the benchmarks, women plaintiffs (victims) were treated more favorably than men, and likewise, male defendants were treated more harshly than their female counterparts. "* The data today is virtually unchanged from coast to coast. Women can get a restraining order with a few words. Men can have visible wounds and still have trouble getting a restraining order. Gynocentrism overpowers justice.

Attorney Sharon D. Liko published an article titled, *"GENDER BIAS YIELDS RESULTS: Restraining Orders handed out to women like candy!"* She is an attorney who works in family court. If anyone can testify of the bias against men, it is her. She states, "Although it is common knowledge that it is a cake walk for a woman to obtain a restraining order against a man if he so much as looks at her cross-eyed, it is virtually impossible for a man to obtain a permanent restraining order against a woman."

She discusses several legal cases that she was personally involved in; cases where men were assaulted by their wife or girlfriend in front of witnesses, and still couldn't get a restraining order. Gynocentrists will never admit that women can be violent. It doesn't fit in with The War on Women. Only the woman can be the victim. No politician or public figure will dare speak out on this. If they do, the Democrats and the mainstream media will quickly accuse them of "hate."

What is most reprehensible is that children are dragged through this mess, are often damaged by it, and the courts are willing accomplices. Two parents are critical to a child's well-being. Yet millions of men have been pushed out of their children's lives by mere allegations or even financial problems.

If any court should be apolitical, it is the divorce courts. The children should come before people's agendas. The judges shouldn't be practicing political correctness at the children's expense. Once again, the evil nature of gynocentrism shows itself. To hell with the children, let them be fatherless and damaged by bigoted courts. The Democratic Party needs votes; that's all that matters.

Case Study: Gynocentrism and Insurance

By now, you see how feminists have made gynocentrism the expected standard. Women are to receive preferential treatment in all areas of life, even insurance costs. For many years, boys have been charged much more for auto insurance. The stereotype is that teenage boys are all drag-racing with sunglasses on, while teenage girls have two hands on the wheel and never go above the speed limit. Well, fasten your seat belt as the real statistics and gynocentrism are exposed once again. But first, an honesty check.

The insurance companies haven't declared a war on boys. Insurance companies will take advantage of anyone they can in order to make a dollar. The reason they charge boys more, **is because they know they can get away with it**! If they charged females more for anything, they would be sued for discrimination.

Here are some statistics from a study on accidents: "The investigators discovered that teenage boys start recklessly, with about 20 percent more crashes per mile driven than teenage girls. Males and females between the ages of 20 and 35 run almost identical risks. Females over the age of 35, however, are significantly more likely to crash than their male counterparts."

Here is another from The University of Michigan that studied 6.5 million car crashes: "Researchers find women are more likely to get into accidents with other women, even though females drive fewer miles than men." The study breaks down accidents into multiple categories, but concludes boldly, "The study shows that women are more likely to cause traffic accidents." Another study by researchers at the John Hopkins School of Medicine and Public Health found that, "Women are more likely to be involved in car crashes than men."

There are far more women over thirty-five driving automobiles than there are teenage boys driving automobiles. What does that mean? It means that female drivers cost the insurance companies far more than teenage boys do. But they are not charged more than male drivers of the same age. Once again, gynocentrism prevails. It is perfectly fine to charge young males more for insurance than young females, because they are a greater risk. But the insurance companies don't dare charge women drivers more for insurance even though they are a greater risk. If they charged women more, they would be sued by the Justice Department for discrimination, and there would likely be a massive penalty imposed by the government. But when boys are charged more, then it is perfectly fine.

It gets even better. Let's talk about health insurance. Women cost the health care system much more than men. Pregnancy and childbirth aren't the only reasons, not by a long shot. Women simply go to the doctor much more than men, and women get sick more often. *Time Magazine*'s Hadley Heath writes, "Women should pay more for health care. Women's costs are higher, and they live longer, yet Obamacare will charge men the same for health insurance premiums. This attempt at fairness is anything but fair. If fairness were really the guiding principle, it would be quite simple: women would pay more for health insurance, because women consume more health care. Women's greater attentiveness to their own health likely also contributes to their longevity. Pregnancy and childbearing aside, women seek preventive care and visit doctors more often.

These additional screenings cost money, and the person receiving the care should pay for it, not other members of her insurance pool (community-rated or not). After all, women may reap the benefits of this behavior by living longer lives; they should also take on the costs. People are uncomfortable in acknowledging sex differences in health care costs, but they should recognize that those same differences crop up in other markets too. It's not discussed as frequently, but sometimes men are the ones paying more for certain purchases, like car insurance. Would it be fair to charge women more for it just to give men a discount?"

Her argument nails the point and challenges gynocentrism. She won't be getting an invitation to speak at the Democratic Party National Convention.

As usual, the Democrats gave the gynocentrists everything they wanted. Even though women cost the health care system more than men, it is now illegal to charge women more for health insurance, courtesy of the Affordable Care Act of 2014. They needed to stop the insurance companies' War on Women. However, not a thing was changed for boys. They will still pay more for auto insurance. What an incredible double standard! Women cost auto insurers more, but only males are charged a higher premium. Women cost the health insurers more, but men are expected to subsidize them with higher premiums. This is the new female-centered America the feminists dreamed of.

Chapter 12: The Real War

The Democrats learned long ago that dividing the people helps win elections. They didn't invent this strategy; it was even used by the Romans under Caesar. If you keep the people divided and fighting amongst themselves, they won't unite for a common cause and put you out of power. So the Democrats pit women against men, black people against white people, rich people against poor people, and religious people against atheists; on and on it goes.

Wherever a wedge can be inserted, they do it. As planned, this leads to social chaos and hatred. In this chaos comes opportunity for them. They ride into town as saviors. Even though they started the hatred, they convince the people only they can "heal the nation" and correct the injustices. But they never correct the injustices they allege.

The last thing the Democrats want is peace and harmony amongst the people. This is why during each and every election they convince people they are a victim of something. And they will fix it. They promise to lift people out of poverty, but after four years, there are just as many people in poverty. They promise to help African Americans. But after four years, the same problems exist for African Americans, particularly in the inner cities (high crime rates, violence, and little opportunity). They promise women they will eliminate the "pay-gap" between the sexes. But as soon as they are elected, they take no action. Can anyone name a legitimate bill put forth by the Democrats to eliminate the pay-gap? They promise to tackle high interest rates for student loans. But after four years, the interest rates are still extortionate. They promise to end wars, but the wars continue when they are in office.

The Democrats don't want these problems to be solved. What would they talk about during each election? If they tell you their true intentions, they can't win. If they say, "We want to take as much of your money as possible to enrich our friends," no one will vote for them.

If you think this is cynical, here's how Washington really works. Every year, the federal government collects trillions of dollars in tax revenue. The states and local governments collect over a trillion also. Can you even write one trillion numerically? Most people don't even know how many zeroes there are. Here it is: 1,000,000,000,000. It takes 1,000 billion to make one trillion. It is an unimaginable amount of money. And many, many politicians have become filthy rich off of this money. This is what they are really fighting for. The politicians decide where the money goes **and who gets it.**

Here is just one of many examples. A billionaire named George Kaiser is known as a top fundraiser for the Democrats. When you bring in money for the party, there are great rewards. Kaiser decided to invest in a solar power company—with your money, of course! He received loan guarantees from the government worth $535 million. When the company went bankrupt, the American taxpayers had to suffer the loss.

Mr. Kaiser is still a billionaire and remains a darling of the Democratic Party. The White House tried to deny influencing this reckless loan, but top fundraiser, George Kaiser, made multiple visits to the White House in the months just before the company was granted a $535 million loan from the government. The Democrats said there was no connection between Mr. Kaiser's visits and the loan, and all the money he brought in had no influence on the decision. One politically connected man cost the taxpayers $535 million dollars.

He is just one of thousands fleecing the taxpayers for their own personal gain. Those who bring in money are known as "bundlers." And when you are a top bundler, the rewards are great. Consider this excerpt from a story in *The Center for Public Integrity,* "Telecom executive Donald H. Gips raised a big bundle of cash to help finance his friend Barack Obama's run for the presidency. Gips, a vice president of Colorado-based Level 3 Communications LLC, delivered more than $500,000 in contributions for the Obama war chest, while two fellow senior company executives collected at least $150,000 more. Level 3 Communications, in which Gips retained stock, meanwhile received millions of dollars of government stimulus contracts for broadband projects in six states—though Gips said he was 'completely unaware' of the stimulus money." Gips raised money for the Democratic Party and then millions of dollars of taxpayer money just mysteriously showed up at his company. Funny, when people don't raise money for the Democratic Party, money never shows up mysteriously.

Again, this is just one more example of one man influencing millions of dollars in taxpayer money. It's one of the main reasons America is so far in debt and heading for bankruptcy in the near future. The real war is against the working class men and women. But if they keep you distracted, you just might forget that fact.

The corruption is so blatant that even longtime allies like Jon Stewart are breaking ranks and speaking out. On a recent episode of *The Daily Show*, here is what happened: "Stewart began his segment by recounting an argument he had gotten into with former House Speaker Nancy Pelosi on his program. Stewart alleged all of Washington was corrupt, while Pelosi said that if it was corrupt, it was only made that way by Republicans. Using the president's recent ambassadorship nominees as an example, Stewart proved Pelosi wrong.

Stewart was fascinated that many of the appointees hadn't even visited their appointed countries, with one alleging he didn't know much about the country he was supposed to act as official liaison to. When trying to determine why some of the nominees could seem so oblivious to their prospective posts, Stewart focused on one very important thing. 'It definitely couldn't be because the new Norway nominee raised $850,000 for Obama's re-election campaign, or the Argentinian one raised $500,000, or the Icelandic one bundled $1.6 million, that would mean that not only would Democrats be seen as corrupt (but Nancy Pelosi told me personally only Republicans are) that Iceland costs like three times more than Argentina,' Stewart said, mocking the Democrat's for their hypocrisy" (Douglas Barclay, writing for *Rare*). As you have seen throughout this book, money is always the motivating factor in Washington, not the people's interests.

If you think these cases are the exception, "More than two years after President Obama took office vowing to banish 'special interests' from his administration, nearly 200 of his biggest donors have landed plum government jobs and advisory posts, **won federal contracts worth millions of dollars for their business interests**, or attended numerous elite White House meetings and social events, an investigation by iWatch News has found."

This is just the President rewarding those who bring in the money, and it cost the taxpayers billions. Now think of every congressman and senator doing the exact same thing all across the country. It isn't the exception at all; when a Democrat *isn't* fleecing the system, that is the exception! The amount of taxpayer money being shifted to politically connected people is destroying us as a nation.

If you think money isn't the major interest of the Democrats, take a look at what some big names have done. Nancy Pelosi has a net worth of between 50-100 million dollars. Here is just one instance of her manipulating taxpayer money for her own good, "For years, Pelosi has pushed for federal transportation earmarks to build and extend a light rail project in her affluent San Francisco district, securing more than $890 million for the project between 2004 and 2011. Interestingly, Pelosi and her husband own an office building, valued between $1 million and $5 million, located at a prime distance from one of the planned light rail stops. If the project is completed, the Pelosis' could see the property value increase by as much as 150%, according to Schweizer" (per *Business Insider*).

During the recession of 2008 through 2011, Pelosi's net worth went up over 50 percent. That's millions upon millions of dollars. Again we see it, one politician steering $890 million in taxpayer money for their own interests. Funny, the rest of the country is suffering in an economic downturn, and politicians see their net worth continue to rise through the roof.

Bill Clinton has made over 100 million dollars from "speeches," since he left office. Why would anyone pay him all this money for just talking? Is he really that interesting? Or, is it payback for dirty deals he made while he was president?

Al Gore has made over 300 million dollars since he left office. Not bad for a single decade. According to *The Telegraph,* "Al Gore, the former US vice-president, is in line for a $30m (£19m) windfall from an Apple share package awarded to him by Steve Jobs, the tech giant's late founder, a decade ago. Under the terms of the award, Mr. Gore was given the right to buy 59,000 Apple shares for $7.475 each. The shares closed at $500 on Friday, meaning his investment has grown from $440,000 to $29.5m in the space of a decade. Mr. Gore is free to sell the shares at any time. Earlier this month, Forbes "conservatively" estimated that Mr. Gore's net worth was at least $300m."

Can you buy $500 per share stocks for $7 per share? Why would Apple founder Steve Jobs just give almost 30 million dollars to Al Gore? What does he know about technology? Gore flunked out of law school and divinity school. But suddenly, he knows so much about technology that Apple is just handing him thirty million dollars for "sitting on the board." Do you believe this? Or do you think he was using his influence in Washington to help Apple's global aspirations? We will never know the truth. All we know is that virtually every Democrat becomes a millionaire "serving the people."

Barack Obama has made over ten million dollars since being elected to public office. "The Center for Responsive Politics analyzed the personal financial disclosure data from 2012 of the 534 current members of Congress, and found that the median net worth for congressional Democrats was $1.04 million" (*Time Magazine*).

Greed isn't exclusive to the Democrats, but what is exclusive to them is incredible hypocrisy. These are the same people who scream, "Get the money out of politics," while at the same time, they're using their status to make as much money as possible.

When you hear the Democrats talk about "financial equality," it really means they get to be millionaires while the people struggle to survive. John Kerry is worth 194 million. The Kennedys are worth many millions.

The point of all these examples is that today's "working class" Democrat is usually a millionaire, and they always get richer in office. Who is the real war against? The real war is against the American people, the workers who slave away at their jobs to barely survive. As the people go deeper in debt to keep their heads above water, the politicians take more and more of their hard earned money to spend on *their* interests, not the people's interests. They live in incredible luxury, always exempting themselves from the burdens of the common man and woman.

They do anything to stay in power and live off the people. They lie, deceive, and pit the people against each other. They take the people's money away from them, and then use it to buy votes, no matter how harmful to the country.

The working class is being suffocated with welfare fraud, disability fraud, EBT card fraud, illegal aliens depleting the safety net money, and the reckless pork-barrel spending in Washington. The people who pay the taxes get no help with their children's college expenses, while the children of those who drain the system can go to school almost free.

Ponder this for a moment: Those who work hard and support the country with taxes get no help. Those who contribute nothing get all the help. This is insanity! You can thank the Democrats for this. And they will never change this injustice, because welfare recipients and illegal aliens vote for them. They don't worry about doing the right thing. They only worry about getting the votes and staying in power.

Most people are opposed to this, regardless of their political background. So how do they get elected? By keeping people's attention focused on other drummed-up issues. Never mind the budget deficit and the fleecing of our country, there's a War on Women. Forget about welfare fraud, discrimination is everywhere. You better vote for us. They pit black people against white people, women against men, the religious against non-believers, and on and on it goes; anything to keep people's attention off of the real issue—the fleecing of America by Washington, D.C. You are nothing more than a source of money to them.

The self-righteous Democrats love to speak out against Wall Street. But behind the scenes, they take money from those very same "evil" banks. They talk about the high student loan rates our children pay, yet do nothing about it. What do you think the bank gave them money for? So that they *don't do anything*!

You can buy a home for 3.5 % interest. You can get a car with 0% interest. But we charge our children 9% interest for an education. What kind of a nation economically enslaves its children as soon as they leave home? Enslaves them for an education they will need to survive? The answer isn't pretty; only the evilest of nations would do this. Only the evilest of politicians would take money from these banks to stay silent.

With all the money Washington wastes on patronage, we could pay off all our children's student loans and change their entire life. The economy would explode with all the new spending. But the banks have bought our politicians, and it will not change. Not until **we** change it! Not a bunch of divided groups only worried about themselves. *We the people* must change it *together*.

Few presidents are loved by Americans of both political parties. Abraham Lincoln was one of them. In one of his most famous speeches, he said, "A house divided against itself cannot stand." He is one of the most influential American presidents in history for a reason. His moral compass and vision of justice for all helped make our nation great. Yes, a house divided against itself cannot stand. We can't have different rights and privileges for one group and not the other; that is a divided house.

One of America's Founding Fathers, Patrick Henry, made the same point. He said, "Let us trust God, and our better judgment to set us right hereafter. **United we stand, divided we fall. Let us not split into factions which must destroy that union upon which our existence hangs.**" Focus on that last sentence—**Let us not split into factions which must destroy that union upon which our existence hangs**. But this is exactly what has happened to us. We have been split into factions. Each faction is jostling for what they want, clawing away at each other in blind selfishness, and disregarding what's best for the nation as a whole. We can't have twenty different versions of America, with everyone claiming they are a victim of someone else.

You cannot grant special rights to one group without taking rights away from another group. It simply can't be done. As Martin Luther King, Jr. said from a jail cell, "Injustice anywhere is a threat to justice everywhere. We are caught in an inescapable network of mutuality, tied in a single garment of destiny. Whatever affects one directly, affects all indirectly."

Whatever we do *does* affect all indirectly. We need to take our country back from corrupt politicians. The politics of hate have to stop for America to recover. Special rights might be working for you right now, but the wind can quickly blow in the other direction. Like it or not, we are all in this together.

A Call to Action

So what do you do now? You have seen the truth thoroughly documented in this book. Do you just give up out of frustration? Do you stick your head in the sand and hope someone else fights Washington for you? It's all hopeless anyway, right? What can you do? You can do a lot! When the Democrats, or any politician, start their campaign of deceit you can shine a spotlight on them.

For one thing, you can pass this book around to as many people as possible. You can encourage others to purchase the book and spread it around. This will stop the War on Women propaganda as soon as it starts. If the American people learn the facts in this book, it will expose the Democrats for who they are and cost them millions of votes. An informed electorate makes better decisions.

Share what you have learned with others. Most people don't know these things. They believe what the media has spoon-fed them for years. This isn't about attacking women and exposing their faults. It's about attacking sleazy politicians and exposing the hateful propaganda they use to divide the country. Educate friends and family with the real numbers. You can help. You can influence the next election.

Take what you have learned and post it on Facebook, share it on Twitter or any other networking site. If you have a blog, share it on there. Call your local radio station, write your local newspaper. These things only take a few moments but can be seen or heard by thousands of people. Yes, your efforts can easily be seen by thousands! Do something.

If you're not willing to fight for the truth, who will be? Do it for the sake of your children or any loved one. Once we let the government re-write reality in one area, they will soon re-write reality in every area. If the government says the sky is purple, we will be powerless to teach our children the truth, because the all-powerful government has spoken. When the government decides no one really owns their home, that we are really just renting from them, and they have complete authority over our property, then what?

You see from the examples above that the truth really does matter. The politicians will never fight for the truth or fix America. They will only fight for votes. The media will never fight for the truth, they are only looking to attract as many viewers as possible no matter how they have to do it. The corporations will never fight for the truth or fix America. They are only concerned with making as much money as possible.

It is the common man and common woman who must fight to take the nation back. The people who work and produce for the country, who pay the taxes and carry all the burdens, the people who actually care about their nation and their neighbors. Change must start from the bottom up. It will not start from the top down. This book will be a shot heard across America. It is my way of fighting back against deceit and hate. Will you fight with me?

www.ingramcontent.com/pod-product-compliance
Lightning Source LLC
Chambersburg PA
CBHW050403290526
45786CB00003B/1113